Premka

White Bird in a Golden Cage

My Life with Yogi Bhajan

Pamela Saharah Dyson

Eyes Wide Publishing
MAUI, HAWAII

Premka: White Bird in a Golden Cage
My Life with Yogi Bhajan

by Pamela Saharah Dyson
© 2019 Pamela Saharah Dyson
Published by Eyes Wide Publishing

Cover: Photo of Premka taken in 1972—unknown photographer

Book Design: Chris Molé, booksavvystudio.com

ISBN: 978-0-578-62188-3

First Edition
Printed in the United States of America

May all beings be happy
And have the causes of happiness.
May all beings be free of suffering,
And the causes of suffering.
May all beings never be apart
From the supreme bliss
Which is without suffering.
May all beings abide in the great equanimity
Which is free from indifference, craving and hostility.

'The Four Immeasurables' from
the teachings of the Buddha

Contents

PART I

---------------- ～ ----------------

I said: What about my eyes?
God said: Keep them on the road.
I said: What about my passion?
God Said: Keep it burning
I said: What about my heart?
God said: Tell me what you hold inside it.
I said: Pain and sorrow.
God said: Stay with it.
The wound is the place
where the light enters you.

~ RUMI

London Layover

*T*HE CRAMPING AND THEN THE HEMORRHAGING *began in mid-air. As I felt the gushing warmth that quickly turned to cold wetness between my legs, my mind raced, trying to make sense of the sheer volume of blood that was suddenly drenching me.*

One empty seat away from me, Yogi Bhajan had been dozing off. My gasp of shock startled him awake. Seeing the panic-stricken look on my face, and then the blood stains appearing through my recently purchased Indian-style pants and shirt, he instantly reached for the overhead call-button while signaling to a nearby stewardess, "Hey, come quickly, there's an emergency over here."

Elegantly wrapped in an Air India uniform sari, the stewardess appeared in the graceful manner of carefully manicured and coiffed Indian women—seeming to float, rather than walk. She instantly assessed my situation, then calmly and efficiently went to gather supplies.

Within a few seconds, to my increasingly foggy consciousness she seemed to glide back into view. She carefully but firmly bundled blankets around me, speaking in proper Indian English, "I have just now spoken to the Captain, and he informs me that we will soon begin our scheduled descent into the London airport. He is calling ahead for an emergency vehicle to meet us as soon as we arrive. No need to worry, doctors will be standing by." I was thankful for her confident reassurances, and for the layers of blankets now protecting me against the frigid temperatures inside this crowded aircraft. In addition to my general shock and confusion, I was feeling light-headed and slightly disoriented.

From what seemed like a far distance, I saw the Yogi nodding reassuringly, mouthing words I couldn't hear as they were drowned out by the persistent drone of the jet engines and the chilling hiss of the overhead vents. But I understood his hand motions—indicating for me to remain calm, to stay quiet, stay still. After more than two years as personal attendant to this larger-than-life spiritual teacher of mine, I understood him intuitively, instinctively. Though I couldn't really hear his words, I knew he was encouraging me to pray, he was instructing me to 'have faith in God.'

It was March of 1971, and we were returning from a nearly three-month visit to India, along with another 83 of his students and followers. Since meeting him in 1968, the summer I turned 25, I had placed myself into the full devotional service of this teacher. I had accepted his challenge to fully surrender my life to serving him and his mission. My years by his side had reinforced my capacity to keep up appearances, to remain graceful under all circumstances. So, breathing deeply and deliberately, I tried to relax, pray and trust.

But a fearsome and nagging thought was there—the fact that two months earlier I had an abortion at a small clinic in India. I wondered if that event might be related to this one? The fact of my pregnancy and subsequent abortion was a secret I knew I must keep in order to protect Yogi Bhajan. After all, he was a spiritual teacher to thousands, and he preached monogamy and abstinence prior to marriage. And he had a wife and three children still residing in India.

An ambulance was waiting to receive me as we landed at Heathrow Airport, London. In the moments when I was conscious, I remember being carried off the plane on a stretcher, and then the sound of the intermittent whaling of a British siren as we raced to nearby Hillingdon Hospital.

It was a short time later when I awoke to find myself in a hospital gown, lying between crisp white sheets. My bed was one of many in a

2

bustling yet hushed Admitting Area. A steady flow of hospital person-
nel moved efficiently around me, as beds were rolled in and out. An
intravenous line was taped onto my left arm, and I was relieved to
see the Yogi grinning at me from the foot of my hospital bed.

However, considering the serious nature of my condition, his grin
seemed incongruent; it seemed to communicate a forced bravado,
an attempt at masking his fear. But I could see it, just below the
surface, because we shared the emotion: fear, that wavered between
the threat of my personal survival and the implications of letting
anyone find out that I had been pregnant. His look was undoubtedly
meant to convey optimism, to reassure me, to persuade me that
everything was going to be alright. I wanted to believe that, but from
my vantage point, things were not looking good.

I was also painfully aware that this man I was in love with,
who was also my spiritual teacher, stood six feet away from me,
not by my side. In my brief lucid moments, it again occurred to me
that it might be helpful for someone in this Emergency Ward to be
informed about my recent medical procedure. I wondered if the
Yogi tell them? Would he allow **me** *to tell them?*

Serving him day and night, I had learned to interpret the Yogi's
use of subtle messages. Now his distance and his body language
seemed intended to communicate to everyone bustling around us
that he was not personally involved with 'this young American
woman'. His posturing implied that he was more of a concerned
bystander, just my spiritual mentor.

Although I understood the reason for such a message, it still
triggered a familiar theme of mine—of being unwanted—my own
issue of being an inconvenient child unexpectedly conceived by
my teenaged parents who were caught up in events leading up to
World War II.

It also presented a mini crisis of faith in my attempt at surren-
dered devotion to this powerful and charismatic Yogi, as I wondered

3

whether the test of my devotion required that I keep this secret, even if it killed me?

In spite of my best efforts to control my doubting mind I had an unwelcome but nagging fear that my teacher might be more concerned about his own image than about my survival. The 'faithful devotee' voice inside my head argued to reconcile this apparent dichotomy, reminding me that as his personal attendant, my life was surely much less important than his.

For the past 2½ years, I had been in nearly constant conflict about the appropriateness of our physical relationship while fulfilling my increasingly prominent role as his most exemplary female devotee. I would remind myself that I'm his student, his devotee. He calls me Premka, which he translates as 'Beloved of God'. He often explains to me that he is above earthly desires. He has assured me that he is simply fulfilling a karmic responsibility to me, that he is 'living three lifetimes in one'. I must believe all of that, because he tells me so. I just wished he would tell me that it's okay to let one of these doctors know about my recent medical history. It could be a matter of life or death! So confusing.

During one of the brief moments when I regained consciousness, the Yogi spoke to reassure me, "These doctors will take good care of you, Premka. I'm grateful to God that He brought us into London at the perfect time. Let us be in gratitude to God and Guru. You must pray, Premka. Remember that your prayer is very powerful."

He had often told me, over the years, that my prayer was very powerful. Really, I wondered? What makes my prayer so uniquely powerful? Because he said it, I tried to take it in, trust that it was so. Lying there, in this London hospital, feeling weak as a kitten, with barely enough energy to speak, I managed to reply, "Yes, Yogiji, I'm praying."

He went on, "Now Premka, I know you understand that I must run to catch the remainder of my flight back to Los Angeles. After all, it's my responsibility to return these students of mine safely back to America. I've been trying to convince these doctors to just let you come along with us, but they won't allow it. I must complete this duty to my students. My son, Vikram Singh, he is living right here in London. Once you are out from the hospital, he has promised me he will look after you. He will take you to the London ashram and make you comfortable until you are ready to fly. Soon you will be joining me in L.A. Just trust in God."

Those were the last words I heard before I faded back into unconsciousness, even as I puzzled over how I had come to be in such a predicament.

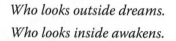

Who looks outside dreams.
Who looks inside awakens.

~ C.G. JUNG

Blossoming Idealism

L IFE CIRCUMSTANCES, MY PERSONAL QUEST, the spiritual high of the '60s and what some would call destiny, all converged to bring about my first meeting with Yogi Bhajan.

It was at the invitation of my high school best friend that I moved from Seattle to Los Angeles in the mid-60s. As I was turning 22 that year, it was my break away from hometown family ties. My choice of L.A. was based on the assumption that Terri and I would take up our relationship where it left off. Instead, I was seriously disappointed to discover that my former best friend was quite busy with a life filled with male suitors and world travels. Terri was an airline hostess for TWA. She was beautiful, brilliant and much more worldly wise than I.

Unexpectedly, I found myself quite alone in a very big city. Still, it was an exciting time to be living in southern California and by 1968 I was employed as an executive secretary at Warner Brothers Records and divorced after a two-year attempt at married life. Although I was technically working within the 'establishment', I was now in the music industry, where the ideals of my baby-boomer generation were being given voice.

I was drawn to the blossoming spiritual idealism of the times. Idealism that included ending the war in Viet Nam, but was also about an awakening consciousness, about living in the recognition of our Oneness.

I wasn't prepared to fully reject middle-class values or to drop out, yet I found my own ways of pursuing the transformative ideals of the time. This included weekly counseling sessions with a pipe-smoking, goatee-wearing therapist who looked to me like Sigmund Freud. I had been part of a circle of acquaintances who used marijuana as a sacrament, as a tool for self-reflection. The woman who facilitated our circle was a social worker herself and she advocated further self-discovery through sessions with her own therapist, Dr. Goldman. My personal decision to enter therapy was further motivated by a continuing discomfort within my own skin and was aimed at identifying and healing my own childhood wounds. With this Jungian therapist and *The Tibetan Book of the Dead*[1] as guides, I took my first consciousness-awakening journey on LSD.

During that same period of time I attended the famous Love-In at Elysian Park. Wandering through the crowds by myself, I came upon amazing musicians who were playing for free, and young people who wore wild tie-dyed clothes, or few clothes, or even no clothes! Complete strangers hugged each other, just because. Love was in the air, while inhibitions were being dropped left and right.

In those years, the last half of the '60s, I was also practicing hatha yoga on a daily basis and reading spiritually enlightening books like *The Way of the Sufi*[2] and *Autobiography of a Yogi*[3] along with the writings of Krishnamurti and C.G. Jung. Following my divorce, I rented a duplex apartment on the side of the Hollywood hills, on Beachwood Drive. I loved driving my little black MG convertible, with the top down, through those hills over my lunch hour and then driving back to work in the Warner Brothers offices in Burbank.

The music I loved was rich with mind-expanding sounds and lyrics that spoke to the issues and angst of my generation:

---

[1] Translation by Walter Evans-Wentz

[2] Author: Idries Shah

[3] Author: Parmahansa Yogananda

Bob Dylan, Joan Baez, Creedence Clearwater, Simon and Garfunkel, et al. Inspired by all of it and impacted by the subtle altered states achieved through yoga and meditation, (and by the not-so-subtle altered states induced by mind-expanding drugs) by late 1968 I concluded that I needed to find my guru.

What I thought I understood about finding a guru (from books!) was that one must be in the right place, at the right time, and in the right attitude or consciousness. I expected that once I found one, it would then be like having my own personal guide through life: an enlightened being who knew the right way to live and who would be dedicated to keeping me on track and safe in a world where the old rules no longer applied. That's what I wanted: some safety and certainty in the midst of all the changing times.

I also feared that, at the ripe old age of 25, and a divorcee at that, I might have missed any chance for the happily-ever-after marriage and family life (my only worldly ambition.) A spiritually dedicated life therefore seemed to be my most desirable alternative. Having long ago rejected the Christian mythology, I was instead attracted to Eastern thought, Eastern practices. I was even drawn to the Eastern musical sounds of the sitar and table. This was the same time period when the Beatles went to India to study with Maharishi, the founder of Transcendental Meditation (TM).

Although I was tempted more than once to just pack it all up and head back to my comfort zone in Seattle, there was more that was compelling me. I was responding to a deep urge to break free of the limitations of old family patterns, to grow beyond the emotional and psychological parameters of my family of origin. I was seeking answers to the age-old questions that had arisen within me: "What is the meaning of life? Who am I and why am I here:"

I was on a quest, one that had been inspired years earlier …

Stand still. The trees ahead and bushes beside you
Are not lost. Wherever you are is called Here,
And you must treat it as a powerful stranger,
Must ask permission to know it and be known.
The forest breathes. Listen. It answers.
I have made this place around you.
If you leave it, you may come back again,
    saying Here.
No two trees are the same to Raven.
No two branches are the same to Wren.
If what a tree or a bush does is lost on you,
You are surely lost. Stand still. The forest knows
Where you are. You must let it find you.

~ *Lost* by DAVID WAGONER

Lake Joy—1956

LAKE JOY WAS SURROUNDED BY THE ABUNDANT evergreen forests of Washington State. It was a small lake, small enough to walk around on a summer morning, or to swim across, with mom or dad as my rowboat escort. Back then, in the mid-1950s, there was a rule that boats with motors larger than 2.5 hp were not allowed on the lake—which kept Lake Joy quiet and peaceful. The simple dirt road that wrapped around the lake was bordered on one side by woods. Thick and tall, I found these woods inviting, full of life, full of mystery and wonder.

Each year, as the season turned to spring, my mom and dad, my younger sister, brother and I, would stock up the family car with food supplies and bathing gear, to drive for an hour and a half to spend a weekend at the family cabin on Lake Joy. It was a tiny, rustic cabin with a barely functional kitchen for mom and enough beds for everyone to sleep. Set a few hundred feet back from the shore of the lake, all the great outdoors was our living room.

On one of those late spring visits to Lake Joy, after a long Seattle winter, I stepped out of our car onto a ground covered with tiny toads. I could not find any inch of earth to step on that was not covered in those tiny creatures, all exactly the same size, shape and color, less than half the size of a dime! I was barefoot, as I often was, and thankfully they all managed to hop around my feet and not under them. One year we were met by a similar groundcover of tiny black spiders and yet another year it was tiny snakes. Each of those plagues, as I called them, created a living, moving carpet across our front yard!

We spent many an idyllic summer weekend there, roasting marshmallows and hotdogs by a campfire, fishing, catching frogs and shooting tin cans with Dad's .22 rifle. I got to be a bit of a tom-boy. I loved rough housing with my dad and my younger brother. We wrestled and boxed with big thick boxing gloves, we fished and we camped. My relationship with my mother was much more challenging. Dad was easier and more fun, and I grew up without any girlish aversions to slimy polliwogs, or to gutting a trout.

One of our best family adventures had to coincide with exactly the right week in spring. This was our annual trek into the woods, to hunt and gather morel mushrooms. These delectable mushrooms grew at the base of a particular tree, one that had whitish bark at the top and that grew tall enough to rise above all the other evergreens. The morel was considered a delicacy and though none of us kids cared to eat them, mom and dad loved them. What I loved was the adventure of hunting for them.

'There's one, dad!' I cried as I spotted the tree with the characteristic features of white bark and fluttering green leaves as it rose above the canopy of the forest. We all took in the sight, and setting his bearings, Dad took the lead as we would dive back through the thick maze of trunks and limbs, ferns and brush to finally arrive at the base of that solitary and special tree.

That was magic all by itself—these spacious, uninhabited forest lands. Empty of people. Full of life, whispering secrets, endlessly.

Sure enough, the ground beneath that tree was loaded with magically proliferating, brain-like mushrooms. Except for those times when the deer had been there ahead of us, leaving only their own black droppings and chewed off mushroom stalks. Still, over the course of a day, we gathered a huge bag filled with edible mushrooms, and then hauled them back to clean and prepare for cooking, with plenty for sharing with friends or to be frozen for future use.

Apart from those group excursions, I sometimes enjoyed my own solitary adventures. One morning, the summer I turned 13, I set out on such a journey. Careful to make note of my point of entry, the direction of the road and the sun's position in the sky, I quietly ventured into the old growth of pine and fir trees.

As the dust-covered edges of the forest were quickly left behind, the flora underwent visual transformation and the many shades of green came more alive. Change came to me as well, as my mind and body settled into the rhythms of nature. The silence was huge—a hush that was at the same time humming with the activities of birds and bees, butterflies and squirrels, rabbits and deer.

I got to be there with them. I felt at home there. The trails I followed were deer trails. The fragrance of cedar and pine mixed with the smell of decomposing vegetation, all warmed and gently lit by sunlight through the boughs and colored by fresh green leaves, wildflowers and wildlife.

I marveled at the forest floor, the soft green carpet of moss that grew over all the old broken branches and chunks of bark that had been shed from the trees. The soft-to-the-touch, fur-like moss covered the process of decay with a fresh, green face, and made a wondrous carpet that silenced the sound of my footsteps, and held me suspended, slightly above the earth beneath.

I had by now explored these woods many times, so it was quite unexpected when, on this particular morning, up ahead I spotted a clearing, a meadow, in the middle of the thick heart of the forest! The sight drew me, invited me forward—and as I approached, I saw that deer were grazing there. I stopped to watch them, dropping down to the moss-covered earth as I instinctively sought to match their stillness, hoping my presence wouldn't frighten them away. Sunlight was streaming into the clearing, filtering through the trees on the perimeter of the meadow, forming distinct rays of gentle light, rays that were alive with tiny beings mixed with nature's dust.

Then it happened—the deer, at virtually the same instant, turned their heads towards me. Tall ears twitching, then stopping still as their eyes met mine across the meadow—all three of them at once.

In that instant, time slowed to Full Presence. The stillness was all-encompassing. The moment seemed infinite, total and spacious:

Silence...

timelessness...

emptiness...

recognition...

acceptance...

oneness...

love that just 'is'.

I could not say how long that moment lasted. But it was full and deep, rich and utterly profound. I had somehow been granted a special insight, a wordless realization about the oneness of all things, about the simple, intrinsic nature of Being, about stillness and emptiness. It seemed to me then that the heavens had opened up, that a doorway to another dimension had been revealed and I had been allowed to see in.

This experience was so sacred to me that I kept it to myself for many years. I felt that any attempt to speak about it would diminish its significance. It touched me so deeply that I spent much of my adult life seeking to understand how it happened, wishing I could make it happen again—and being indelibly imprinted with the insights it gave me.

In Search of My Guru

M Y SERIOUS SEARCH FOR A GURU began at HELP Restaurant. In 1968, this was one of the first vegetarian restaurants in Los Angeles. Searching the postings on their public bulletin board, I was awe-struck by an 11"x14" poster featuring a photo of Swami Satchidananda. His radiant, glowing face was mystically suspended, without displaying any supporting body parts, in sepia tones against an ivory-colored background. His elegant facial features were perfectly framed by his thick, shoulder-length, grey-streaked hair and flowing beard. He looked omniscient, pure, wise, and illuminated from within. His eyes were alive, his smile inviting. Incredulously, I wondered: *Is it possible that such a guru, such a spiritual teacher, could be found right here, right where I live? Is it possible I could actually find someone like this?* I could barely imagine it. I had assumed I would need to travel to distant exotic places to find someone as magnificent as he. As it turned out, the poster was promoting a presentation, not by the Swami himself, but by one of his students.

Then I spotted another announcement, about a Sufi teacher named Pir Vilayat Inayat Khan[4], who would be lecturing at the East-West Cultural Center of Los Angeles over the weekend. I decided to be there!

I arrived early at the East-West Cultural Center and claimed a seat near the front of the lecture hall. I wanted to have a close-up

---

4   A teacher of meditation and the traditions of the East Indian Chishti Order of Sufism.

experience of this real, live spiritual teacher from the East. When Pir Vilayat arrived on the small stage, he took his seat upon a kind of throne, facing toward the audience. He was briefly introduced, and we were all instructed to sit quietly, while he continued to sit with his eyes closed, never looking up at the attendees. Eager to hear the wisdom I expected would come pouring forth from him, I sat as instructed for several minutes, then impatiently opened my eyes to see if he was ever going to speak.

Now that my eyes were open, I was surprised to see that Pir Vilayat was fidgeting (not just a little, but a lot!) as he seemed to try to find some ease, some comfort in his own skin. Even as he squirmed, his eyes remained closed, as though to imply that he was meditating. But his eyes weren't just closed, they were squeezed shut, like he was defending against something he didn't want to see. Or maybe he was experiencing pain that he was struggling to contain?

What did this have to do with spiritual teachers or gurus, or the enlightenment I was seeking? I wondered. I looked around the room at the people seated behind me, to see how others were responding. Everyone else had their eyes closed, and no one seemed to notice this strange dichotomy of a spiritual teacher, a guru, who was so apparently uncomfortable in his own skin.

Now that I was so distracted, I continued to scan the audience until I noticed a tall impressive figure standing at the rear of the hall. A bright pink turban crowned the head of a dark-complexioned man, with a jet-black, short and curly beard. Like me, his eyes were not closed, as he was also surveying the audience. His features were strikingly handsome, his well-proportioned face accentuated by sparkling black eyes—eyes that met mine briefly, across the crowded hall.

Though he was dressed in casual western-style clothes, from the neck up he looked as though he might have stepped right out of *The Arabian Nights.* Even at this distance, Yogi Bhajan had a magnetic energy. The charisma, the draw, seemed tangible. During my recent search of that bulletin board, I had been told by the owner of HELP Restaurant that an East-Indian man called Yogi Bhajan was teaching yoga classes right here, at the East-West Cultural Center. I guessed that this must be him.

Pir Vilayat did finally speak, though he never did open his eyes. I had come with high expectations, assuming there would be some dynamism, some life-altering wisdom, some fireworks going off around him. But that didn't happen for me.

Disappointed, I got up to leave, moving toward the exit at the rear of the room, jostling along in the aisle at the pace of the crowd, as many stopped to exchange greetings and converse with one another. I didn't know anyone else in the room, and although I felt curious about the Yogi and could have gone up to speak with him, my insecurity and hesitation won out. It seemed so unlikely that such an exotic-looking being would be approachable, that he would have any interest in speaking to me. Besides, I wondered, *what would I say to him?* I slipped out of the hall and thoughtfully drove back home.

"Oh my God, he is s-o-o-o sexy!" Jan gushed to me over the phone a few days later.

I couldn't believe it! Jan was my less-than-five-foot tall, doe-eyed, curvaceous and adorable best friend. I had shared with her about my first sighting of Yogi Bhajan. Now she had beaten me to it—she had gone ahead and taken a class with him.

She continued to fill me in, enthusiastically running all of her words and sentences together, "He's from India, and he wears this steel bracelet on his wrist that he says can be used as a weapon to defend himself (or women and kids and old people) and it's also some kind of religious symbol." She continued, breathlessly, "He says his hair is really long because in his religion they don't believe in cutting hair. He says that's why he wears the turban—to keep his long hair clean and protected. I don't think he's very old, and he doesn't wear a wedding ring. I really liked his class. You should definitely call and make an appointment."

Well, I thought, that's easy enough for her to say. After all, Jan was happily married to her bodybuilding, brandy-sniffing, childhood sweetheart. With the security of her visible wedding ring and big strong David in the background, she had been bold enough to check out Yogi Bhajan.

Being a recent divorcee, I felt much more vulnerable. In that era, there were silent assumptions about women who had been married and divorced—they were clearly no longer virgins, so they had a bit of a stigma. But it was motivating to me that she had gone ahead, while I had hesitated. It also confirmed to me that he was *available*, he's a teacher who's right here in L.A. If Jan could take a class with him, then so could I.

Within minutes of hanging up from that conversation, I was dialing the East-West Cultural Center. It only rang twice before I was surprised to have it answered by a male with a thick East-Indian accent—the Yogi himself! Feeling flustered at this unexpectedly close encounter, I managed to let him know that I was calling because I was interested in taking a private yoga class.

"Ah, you want to study yoga? Well, what kind of yoga do you want?" With a singsong and rapid-fire delivery, the Yogi continued without a pause, "You want Raja Yoga/Bhakti Yoga/ Karma Yoga/ Hatha Yoga/ Tantra Yoga / Kundalini Yoga?"

He quickly rattled off this string of slightly familiar terms ... and I didn't have a clue how I was supposed to answer such a question! So I rather flippantly responded, 'All of them, I guess.'

The institutional-green walls, the gently swishing uniforms of nurses and attendants gradually came back into focus, as I once again regained consciousness. I was still lying there in that London hospital, in a busy Emergency Admitting area. But now the Yogi was gone. I reasoned that he was already flying back to California with his other 83 students. I managed to lift the crisp white cotton top-sheet in time to see a fist-sized clot that had just emerged onto the protective sheeting beneath me. I was still hemorrhaging, and now I was all alone

A nurse was hovering nearby, with concern written across her face. I signaled for her to come over and spoke in a weak but clear voice, "I thought you should know that I recently had an abortion, in a small clinic in New Delhi, India."

With the Yogi absent, his involvement was no longer an issue and this new piece of information seemed to be what the doctors needed. Within minutes I was wheeled into surgery, where I was anesthetized into unconsciousness.

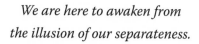

*We are here to awaken from
the illusion of our separateness.*

~ THICH NHAT HANH

The Yoga Class that Rocked My World

W HEN I ARRIVED, TOWARD THE END OF 1968, for my first private yoga class with Yogi Bhajan, he again surprised me by personally greeting me at the main entry door of the East-West Cultural Center, "Ah, you must be Pamela. Come along up to the office. I am just now wanting to interview you."

Interview? Why do I need to be interviewed to take a yoga class? I wondered, while I nonetheless felt compelled by the sheer dynamism of his presence, to follow him up the single flight of stairs.

The East-West Cultural Center was a fairly small but dignified institution, with two large meeting halls, offices and an extensive library. Its wall-to-wall shelves held a treasure house of Eastern philosophical writings. The primary patrons of the East-West Cultural Center were middle-aged or older, very establishment types that we came to call swami-chasers—people with the money and the inclination to sponsor teachers from Eastern traditions. It was a decidedly pre-New Age venue. Having a basic trust in institutions, the studious environment gave me a kind of validation of this overwhelmingly charismatic and surprisingly unconventional Yogi. (His bearing and his demeanor were so regal and impressive that it seemed to me that he should have attendants or secretaries rather than performing mundane tasks like answering telephone calls or acting as his own receptionist.)

Arriving at a small office at the top of the stairs, he directed me to sit in a simple wooden chair directly across from him. Then he began his line of questioning, turbaned head tilted to one side,

"I'm just wondering, Pamela, what kind of work you do?"

Still feeling intimidated by his powerful presence, I haltingly replied, "I'm a secretary. Right now I'm working as an executive secretary at Warner Brothers Records."

"Aha, you are a secretary, I see. So tell me, have you ever studied yoga before?"

Although I was generally inclined to uncertainty and self-consciousness, his simple and straightforward questions put me more at ease about this interview as I replied, "Yes, actually I have been taking hatha yoga classes with an Indian teacher named Bhupesh Guha, for more than a year."

His face showed surprise as he inquired further, "I see. And so why you have come to me?"

It was a very logical question, to which I easily responded, "Well, I wanted to learn more than just physical postures. I've been reading about meditation and sometimes after my yoga exercises, I feel very calm and still. It seems like I must be meditating, but I'm not sure what to do. I want to learn the right way to meditate and I want more *spiritual* instruction. My hatha yoga instructor only teaches the yoga postures."

The six-foot-two-inch tall Yogi wasn't interviewing me from any application form, and he wasn't writing anything down. He was casually straddling the corner of a desk, facing toward me, with one foot securely on the ground, hands folded and resting in his lap. He was wearing a dark coral-colored turban, some khaki-colored slacks and a short-sleeved turquoise shirt tucked into a belted waistband that was pulled tight, causing the slacks to gather around his waist. On his large and well-proportioned feet, he wore loafers, without socks.

All of his questions were basic and they were about me, so I began to feel more at ease as I continued, "Actually, I really wanted to go to India, to find my guru. But I'm afraid to travel there alone.

I've heard stories about Western women being kidnapped and sold into the white slave trade. So I'm thinking I'll go to Europe instead, and I'm hoping I can find my guru there."

The Yogi smiled and nodded thoughtfully, "Ah, yes, I think that is a much better plan. But I have another idea—first you should let me train you as a yoga teacher. That way you can just travel in Europe with respect. You can safely travel to different countries, staying at yoga ashrams wherever you go."

That was a totally unexpected suggestion. I stammered a reply, "Well, that does sound a-a-a- interesting! But I don't really think that I'll have time to learn to be a teacher because I'm planning to leave very soon. How much time would it take?"

He answered without any hesitation, "Ah, this depends on you. It could take a short time, or a little longer time. But if you work hard then it can be done sooner. And you already have experience. So, I will agree to train you, but there is one condition: you must agree to complete the course."

I wasn't yet taking this yoga teacher idea seriously, so I repeated, "But I'm planning to leave for Europe very soon. I've already applied for my passport. Do you really think you can train me to be a teacher so soon?"

He lifted his hands with palms open and shrugged his shoulders in a posture that implied uncertainty, saying, "That's totally up to you. I can teach you. Simply you must promise that you will complete the course." He then reached out his hand, as though to seal an agreement.

It sounded like a good plan, this suggestion he was offering. I really appreciated the idea of safety and respectability while adventuring alone to unfamiliar countries. And at the same time, I was drawn to the Yogi's magnetic presence. I was amazed at what he was suggesting and offering to me, and I couldn't help but be curious to see who he was, this Yogi Bhajan.

Still, I did notice there was a catch; he was asking me to make a promise. And he was offering no timeline for completion, nor any definition of what it would require to 'complete the course'. Nonetheless, his magnetism and his self-assuredness were persuasive, and my youthful naiveté prevented me from challenging any discrepancy. I was fascinated, curious, and even hopeful that maybe he was the spiritual teacher I was looking for. I tentatively extended my hand and replied, "Okay, I would like to be a yoga teacher. I will agree to complete the course."

He looked into my eyes and taking hold of my hand, he challenged my resolve with one word: "Promise?"

Filled with more questions than answers, I nonetheless responded, "Okay, I promise."

Yogi Bhajan then led me back down the stairs, into a large, high-ceilinged and mostly empty meeting hall. At the far end of the room, a young red-headed woman was seated on the floor, stretching into yoga postures. She was apparently practicing routines the Yogi had given her earlier, as he took a moment to encourage her before beginning to direct me through a series of postures. After about 40 minutes of following his instructions, he guided me into a seated, cross-legged position, my upper body bent forward, my forehead touching the ground with my arms stretched above my head with palms together, as he explained, "This posture is called *guru pranam*. Now just hold the pose and breathe long and slow. And remember, no getting up until I say."

I listened attentively to his instructions, settling into the posture, forehead to the floor. Then ... I heard the opening and closing of a door!

Oh my God! Did Yogi Bhajan just go out that door? Did he actually leave the room, with me in this posture?!!! I wanted to call out to him, "Where are you going, why are you leaving me here like this?" After all, it was very confining in this posture and the discomfort in my knees and hips was already building. Plus, I couldn't see anything with my forehead pressed to the floor. I could just barely peek around to the right and the left, at ground level. But there was no sign of the Yogi anywhere!

So, it must be a test, I reasoned. His instruction had been very explicit, 'No getting up until I say.'

I had come in search of the kind of teacher I had read about in books, the kind of enlightened master who tests your sincerity, your obedience and your devotion. *That's how it works!* That's how the teacher determines your readiness: "When the student is ready, the teacher will appear." I wanted to demonstrate that I was ready. So I held the posture, for what seemed to be a really long time... probably 10 long minutes.

Ah, finally I heard the door open. Thankfully, I heard him speaking to me, "Very good, Pamela. This posture just calms the mind. You have done it very well. Now just come lying onto your back, and totally relax." He was now sitting cross-legged on the floor next to me, and it was a great relief to just un-bend my knees, stretch out my legs, and lie flat.

But relaxing would have been a whole lot easier... if he hadn't put his left hand on my right breast!

The really strange thing about his hand on my breast, apart from the fact that it was there at all, was that it seemed to be sort of clinical. He wasn't fondling me, rather his hand was just there. I attempted to remain calm and unruffled, afraid to insult him with an accusation. I didn't want to alienate him before I even got to know who he was. I did manage to sneak a quick peek and saw that he wasn't even looking at me. His hand was just there, on my right breast, while he sat very erect, eyes intently staring off into space, his other hand on my lower abdomen. He seemed to be meditating, deeply contemplating something about me. Once again, I didn't know what to make of him. *It must be another test.* I had read so many stories about the tests of faith, tests of devotion that gurus use to determine the sincerity of their students. I was doing my best to follow the examples portrayed in the books I had read.

He soon removed his hands and seemed to instantly shift from a trance-like state back into ordinary consciousness, as he announced, "We are complete. Best if you come at least two times per week."

It was a bright and sunny day in Southern California, as he walked me toward the main door of the Center. Then he directed me to follow him to a library, where he reached up to a shelf and pulled out a large volume, showing me a prayer entitled *Jap-ji.* It was written in an Indian script with English translations beneath. "I am just requesting if you can type up this English translation for me? I want to make a pamphlet to distribute to my students. You are a secretary, so I am thinking this could be easy for you, to just type it up?"

This Yogi is full of surprises! I was flattered to think that I had some skill he might find valuable, so I assured him that I could do that for him. He then walked me back to the front of the building and with a casual gesture of his arm, encouraged me to follow him across the street, saying, "Come along with me and just meet some of my students. They are all renting apartments in my same building, so they can just study with me."

It was the middle of the day, so I calculated that it was safe as I followed him across the street to a simple brick apartment building. We climbed up the cement staircase to the second floor and into a dimly lit hallway, where we soon came to an open apartment door. There I was introduced to the first student, a man named Wallace. Exceptionally polite and respectful, Wallace was a bearded African American who appeared to be in his early thirties. Then we walked along to another open door where I met Terry, a young Canadian woman in her late teens. Terry was in the midst of straightening up the Yogi's personal apartment and I learned that she had driven all the way from Toronto, to continue to study with 'the Yogi', as she called him.

Then, within minutes, and as if on cue, another of his students appeared, bringing a special salad for the Yogi's lunch. Pulling her by the ear in a playful and mischievous manner, and calling her 'my little thing', he introduced her: "Shakti Parwha is the name I have given her, and it means Great Flow of Divine Energy."

Shakti stood about 5'1", with dark gray, curly hair in a very short, pixyish cut. She was wearing a turquoise blue, single piece jumpsuit with pant legs down to the middle of her calves. In contrast to these other students I was meeting, Shakti had a distinctly middle-aged demeanor. She was what I would call 'straight', pretty much the opposite of 'cool'. She was from another generation though she was clearly a bundle of energy and bristling with self-importance.

I wasn't sure why I had been invited to meet everyone, but it did put me more at ease about the Yogi. I sensed the family feeling between all of them, and the deference and care they were giving to the man they all clearly regarded as their spiritual teacher.

When you follow the crowd you lose yourself.
But when you follow your soul
you will lose the crowd.
Eventually your soul tribe will appear.
But do not fear the process of solitude.

~ Tribe of Amazon, Brazil

Danger: Explosives

IT WAS JUST A FEW DAYS LATER, on a Saturday morning, when my phone rang. Picking it up, I instantly recognized the Yogi's thick East-Indian accent and unique sentence structure, "Eh, good morning, Pamela, you know who is this?"

Containing my surprise, I calmly replied, "Yes, of course I do."

With a bit of a chuckle, he proceeded, "I'm thinking it's such a beautiful day, is it not? And I just had an idea that you might like to come with me on a picnic?"

Surprise, surprise. His voice, his thick accent, his invitation, all set off a cascade of mixed thoughts and feelings. *Was this exotic, tall, dark and handsome Yogi asking me out? Was it a date? Was he interested in me on a personal level? That could make for complications.* In my executive-secretarial career, I had already been instructed in the basic rule that personal relationships are best kept separate from professional ones.

I can't really imagine that he is interested in me. But why would he be calling me, why would he be asking me to go on a picnic? Such thoughts and questions were clamoring for answers as I weighed this unusual invitation. The cultural and language barriers, combined with his spiritual status, his mature age (he was nearly 40), and his overall powerful charisma and outstanding good looks, were intimidating. Perplexed, but more than a little curious, I replied, "Yes, sure, I would like to go on a picnic." After all, a picnic seemed like a very safe way to get to know him and his intentions.

He continued, "I think perhaps you're knowing some nearby park we can visit. I'll just come for you. Here is Wallace. Please just speak with him and tell him the directions, and I will see you at about noon."

Recently divorced from a brief two-year attempt at married life, I had just moved into this cozy little Beachwood Drive duplex in the Hollywood Hills. I had painted my living room walls a deep and vibrant shade of rust/orange, and dedicated the single bedroom as my art studio, where I experimented with pencil drawing, charcoal, and watercolors. A full-sized mattress and box springs served as the main piece of furniture in the living room and was covered with a thin cotton Indian paisley spread, and some throw-pillows. A round, glass swag-lamp hung above one corner of that small room, and a rattan basket chair was suspended near the shuttered windows, alongside a bookcase. My stereo record player, speakers and record albums took up most of one wall.

In addition to the popular music of the '60s, I had a small collection of Eastern classical or world-beat sounds, so there were also albums of Ravi Shankar and Ali Akbar Khan as well as indigenous recordings on the Nonesuch label from places like Bali or the Zen monasteries of Japan. Seemingly familiar to me on some ancient, core level, I felt a great affinity with Eastern rhythms and instrumentations, as I also discovered that they enhanced my meditative states.

This little duplex apartment, nestled on the side of a steep cliff in the Hollywood Hills, represented a new beginning for me where I was setting out to explore my creativity and establish a quiet place to practice yoga and meditation.

It was shortly after noon when I heard the knock on my door. Expecting to see the Yogi, I was surprised and momentarily puzzled when instead I came face-to-face with his student, Wallace. I automatically looked past him, to the driveway down below, and saw the Yogi grinning up at me, leaning casually against the passenger door of a turquoise and white 1960 Chevy. I could also see that Shakti was behind the steering wheel and two other young women were waving to me from the back seat.

Okay, I guess that answers that question—this is not a date! At least it's not like any ordinary date. So, what was the point of this invitation?

Only the Yogi knew the answer to that question, and I wasn't about to embarrass myself by asking. After all, I felt presumptuous to even consider that this really exotic being, this tall, dark and handsome Yogi would have any personal romantic interest in me! I climbed into the car with everyone else as I directed them to nearby Bronson Park, located the next canyon over from mine. After parking the car, we found a grassy spot under a shady canopy of California pepper trees. I looked on as these students of the Yogi spread out blankets, set out food and busied themselves with preparations.

I had been enrolled in photography classes for a few months now and made it a practice to take my camera everywhere. People, faces, spontaneous portraits, were my favorite subjects. Through the lens of my 35mm Olympic camera, I contemplated this odd little grouping of people, a mishmash of ages and ethnicities. Terry was an auburn-headed, cute but still teen-aged and pimple-faced Canadian girl, on the plump side. Wallace was a 30-something, bearded dark-skinned man who worked in an upscale Beverly Hills men's clothing store. His hair and beard were well manicured, and he was casually but neatly dressed. I noticed that his eyes were always averted as he maintained a disciplined and respectful demeanor toward each of us. Shakti was a career waitress with tom-boyishly short gray hair and a rather prominent and unflatter-ing curvature to her upper back—her shoulders rounded forward, effectively concealing any indication of breasts. I sensed that she felt a need to hide them, that she was not comfortable with her own femininity. She struck me as someone who had never been anything other than middle-aged though I learned that she was only a few months older than the Yogi.

By contrast, the Yogi seemed to defy any age or classification.

Then there was Suzy, the golden and freckled redhead from my first yoga class. Also in her teens, she radiated a warm glow, with makeup-free and gentle hazel eyes that were nearly always shyly averted. Suzy was perpetually smiling, sweet looking, heavy breasted and softly cushioned by her extra pounds.

While they were all busy preparing food and serving it up on paper plates, I was capturing this little event on camera, including some stunning shots of the highly photogenic Yogi. After shooting a number of pictures, and once we all had eaten a variety of vegetables, and fruit salads, the Yogi asked me, "Eh, Pamela, can you just show me how to take a snap with your camera?" I pre-set the aperture opening and the shutter speed, showing him how to focus the lens while looking through the viewfinder. He played with it a while, taking a few 'snaps', then he began to direct me, "Eh, Pamela, you just go stand over there, and let me snap your photo." He was pointing for me to go across from the grassy slope where we had set out our blankets. There was another gently sloping hillside with some kind of bunker set into it, with an entrance formed by upright wooden beams, and a horizontal one that capped an opening that had been boarded shut. The Yogi directed me towards that entryway.

The photo he took that day was priceless. It displayed some irony and the Yogi's personal sense of humor: a young blonde American woman wearing a mini-skirt and a Victorian style high-necked blouse, with one arm outstretched, hand pressed against a vertical beam, with one knee bent in a faintly glamorous angle that was accentuated by medium high heels and pantyhose (wouldn't go anywhere without them!) My face was youthful, radiant, smiling. Paradoxically, directly over my head was a crudely executed sign that read: 'Danger: Explosives'.

The portrait I captured of the Yogi was also revealing. His beard was pitch black (with not a hint of gray), curly and glistening in the brilliant autumn sunlight of southern California. He wore a bright watermelon-colored turban, a white long-sleeved crew-neck sweater and khaki slacks, along with those same loafers without socks. He was trim, well-proportioned, with no sign of a belly, thanks to a recent 40-day fast. He stood casually, arms hanging at his sides with his hands gently clasped behind him. His smile seemed a bit forced, almost mocking, and his cheeks were round and full. His eyes were laughing too, with a flash of mischief, while his head gently rocked from side to side.

It was over the course of that casual little picnic that I learned the Yogi had classes at other locations around L.A., and that he didn't drive. I also learned that he was married, with his wife and three children still living in India.

That seemed to answer my question about his intentions. Yet I observed that he didn't seem like any married man I had ever met—rather he seemed utterly unencumbered, very free. *Different. Very different.*

I awoke to the now-familiar bustle of nurses and attendants moving thoughtfully and deliberately through the hushed corridors of this London hospital. Turning my head to my left, I saw that an intravenous line was still taped to my arm, though I sensed the bleeding had virtually stopped. Within moments, a doctor was there, explaining to me in his British accent, "Miss Kaur, your surgery went very well. We simply performed a

D & C⁵, which involves the scraping of the walls of the uterus. The hemorrhaging was your body's attempt to eliminate some tissue left attached to the uterine wall. Now it is all clear so you should have no further difficulties. We are pleased to assure you that there has been no permanent damage, so you are still capable of bearing a child."

That should have been good news, but it reminded me of the painful reality that I was still struggling to accept. The Yogi had been telling me for these months and years, "Premka, it is not in your destiny, in this lifetime, to marry or have a child. You must clear your karma, by just washing my floors, doing my laundry. That is what is required. I'm sorry to tell you this, but that is the Will of the God and I cannot change it."

I broke into tears the first time he told me this. Up to that moment, my only worldly ambition was to fall in love, get married and have children. Giving up this dream seemed to be the ultimate sacrifice.

---

⁵ A dilation and curettage procedure (D&C) in which the cervix can be scraped with a curette to remove abnormal tissues

A Purple Aura

IN THE WEEKS FOLLOWING THAT PICNIC, I learned that Shakti often served as the Yogi's driver, and now I was frequently invited to ride along with them to Claremont Colleges, where he held well-attended classes in a large, open Student Lounge. About 60-100 students would regularly attend those classes, and he often asked me to demonstrate the postures, the mudras and the breathing techniques. Although he spoke fluent English, his accent was still very strong, and I would sometimes help to interpret him for those who couldn't grasp a word or phrase. During the hour-long drives, he would ask me all kinds of questions about the habits and behaviors of Westerners and about my own personal history.

During those first weeks, I was perfectly content with my semi-private yoga classes, even though the Yogi kept encouraging me to attend his meditation classes on the weekends. I was not at all interested in group events, but one weekend he was particularly insistent that I should attend a class he was leading on a Sunday morning, at the East-West Cultural Center.

Arriving a few minutes late, I walked into a hall that was nearly filled to capacity with close to 100 people. Outstandingly, on this particular day, the majority of those present were long-haired hippies, who seemed to have come prepared with their own personal rugs, mats or cushions to allow them to sit cross-legged on the hardwood floor. Many wore cloth bags or knitted holsters which held wooden flutes or tambourines or harmonicas. In contrast, along the outside perimeters of the room, there were a few dozen middle-class, middle-aged regular attendees of the Center, all seated upright on straight-back folding chairs.

As I learned later, on this particular weekend, an entire hippie commune from New Mexico, calling themselves the Jook Savages, had formed a caravan of vans and painted buses, driving into Los Angeles to begin to study kundalini yoga with the Yogi. Clearly, the word was spreading about this tall, turbaned Yogi.

He looked especially brilliant and holy on this day. It was the first time I had seen him dressed all in white, wearing an Indian-style shirt (kurta), made of a thin white cotton with slits at the sides. It hung loose and reached just past the top of his thighs. His legs were fully covered by white cotton pants (churidars) that gathered around his ankles, and he wore some black slippers embroidered with golden threads and with toes that curled up, like shoes a Genie might wear. He also wore a woven purple and magenta shawl, draped loosely around his shoulders while his turban was a deep shade of pink.

Although I was feeling rather out of place in this room full of hippies and middle-aged swami-chasers, I was nonetheless fascinated with what the Yogi was saying, so I remained in the back of the hall. As I listened to his instructions for concentrating on the breath and the use of mantra for focus, his words seemed to transport me, guiding me into a meditative or altered state of consciousness.

It was then that I unexpectedly witnessed a unique phenomenon: a circular band of purple color had materialized around the Yogi's head. I had never seen anything like this, and what was even more surprising to me was the fact that this band of color did not appear to be transparent. It was not ethereal. It seemed to be very solid, like it could have been cut out of cardboard or metal or wood. I blinked, I squinted, I shook my head. I looked around that gathering to see if anyone else was noticing this strange phenomenon. But everyone else was simply sitting there with their eyes closed—while no matter what I did, that circular aura remained there, purple and solid-looking.

From all of my reading, I knew about auras. The Yogi had also spoken about them, claiming, "I sometimes cannot see the person at all. I only see the colors of the aura, not the person. This is why I cannot be fooled by anyone, because the aura tells me the 'inside' story."

I guessed this was what I was seeing, though I had never seen one before. Yet I expected an aura would be translucent, like a rainbow, or like the glowing halo frequently portrayed around the head of Christ or of angels.

I was being shown the Yogi's aura, and it was a beautiful, bright purple color. Solid. I had been deeply questioning whether this Yogi was my guru, whether he was the spiritual guide and protector I had been seeking. Now this mystifying experience seemed to be a confirmation that Yogi Bhajan was not an ordinary man, even as I wondered, *How did he do that?*

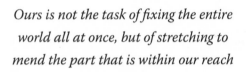

*Ours is not the task of fixing the entire
world all at once, but of stretching to
mend the part that is within our reach*

~ CLARISSA PINKOLA ESTES

Meltdown at Melrose

MY LIFE OUTSIDE OF WORK at Warner Brothers Records was rapidly being swept up in the energy and excitement of Yogi Bhajan's well-attended yoga classes and in his message to his youthful followers. In addition to Claremont College and the East-West Cultural Center, he also taught classes at the YMCA, and in a conveniently located antique and import furniture store on Melrose Avenue, which was owned by one of his students named Jules Buccieri.

The Yogi was teaching much more than just yoga postures. He taught the yogic sciences of postural alignment and the significance of the meridians and energy flows of the body. He taught about the use of food for health and for healing, including advocating vegetarianism, "We do not eat the flesh of the dead animals. These animals die in slaughterhouses, filled with fear. You eat the animal and you take that fear into your own body. Remember, you are what you eat."

He taught about living a dedicated life, with a balance between work and worship. His teachings were drawn from his native East Indian culture, and he combined streams of yoga philosophy, Ayurvedic medicine and the philosophy and spiritual principles of his own Sikh religious tradition. For all of us, this information was totally new, and he seemed to be an endless fountain of knowledge.

In his yoga classes, he combined traditional hatha yoga postures with an energizing breathing technique he called breath-of-fire, his own term for the yogic breath traditionally known as bastrika. He introduced mantras drawn from the Sikh scriptures, combining them with breathing techniques and instructing us in how to use them as the mental focus for meditation.

Within my first weeks of meeting him, he instructed me, "You must rise up in the early hours of the morning, in the Amrit Vela (the hours before the rise of the sun, before the busy-ness of the day) and recite this mantra: Ek Ong Kar Sat Nam Siri Wahe Guru[6]. This mantra will just liberate you from the cycle of karma. You must recite it with the conscious breathing and with the 'locks', the *bhandas*, for two-and-a-half hours each day. If you can just do this for 40 days, then that is all you need. You will be liberated."

Virtually overnight, as I followed his instructions, I gave up smoking (I had been exposed to the second-hand smoke of my parents since infancy, and by the age of 14, I had taken up smoking myself.) I stopped drinking any alcohol or smoking marijuana and stopped eating meat. It all happened effortlessly as Yogi Bhajan and the growing community of students around him filled my life with spiritual practices, techniques and teachings. All of my available time was effectively consumed with attending his classes throughout L.A. I also finished typing up those pages of 'Jap-ji' and making them into pamphlets for distribution to his students.

One evening, toward the end of 1968, I sat in a crowded hall at the transformed furniture store on Melrose Avenue. The display furniture had been moved to outside patios to create enough space for that evening's class. On this particular night there was a larger-than-normal crowd, of more than a few hundred students. The message had been passed along, by word-of-mouth, that there was to be a celebratory feast to follow the always-inspiring lecture. The evening had been declared by the Yogi to be a celebration of an astrological alignment that he told us was heralding the Dawning of the Age of Aquarius.

---

[6] Translation: There is One Creator of all the creation, whose identity is Truth. Great is this wisdom.

That night the Yogi spoke in a thundering voice, his words prophetic sounding, as he declared, "I have come to the west at this crucial time in the evolution of human consciousness. Do not misunderstand, I'm just a humble channel, and I have been sent by my master, to train you to be the teachers who will lead the Aquarian Age. Remember, I'm telling you that I did not come here to collect disciples. I am just here to carve you out to be the leaders of tomorrow. We are witnessing the dawning of a New Age and you are the ones who must carry the message. Whatever happens to me is not important, I'm just following the instructions of my master, to remind you of your destiny and to push you to step up, to take the leadership that is required to guide the humanity toward the God-consciousness."

The packed room grew totally silent, as everyone drank in his words and the future he was describing. His words seemed to prophesy a dream that was already alive in my heart. Then he spoke of his own fate in this exalted vision he was sharing:

"I also want to warn you that I may not live that long. I have seen that time will come when I will be misunderstood, and I may be crucified. That is to be expected. It is part of the destiny of all those who offer themselves to serve the humanity. I understand there will be many conflicts along the way. Some of you will question me, you will doubt me and even some of you will betray me. I'm ready for that, I'm prepared to walk this lonely path. I have even seen that vision—that my back will look like one big scab from all the stab wounds that I'll receive. But I'm ready for this, and I have faith that my guru is always with me."

His delivery was awe-inspiring, and his words were so powerful they seemed to crack me wide open. As I listened intently, they triggered an internal vision, even as I looked around the room that was filled to overflowing with mostly young, radiant and inspired faces. Almost everyone filling that room and standing in the doorways,

41

had long hair, many of the men with youthful beards and all were clearly enthralled with the Yogi's words.

Yet even as I looked at their real-life, glowing faces, I was 'seeing' a future scenario—where many of these inspired students would be disillusioned and leave this teacher. I was literally shown that they would each be challenged and tested and many of them would doubt him and finally abandon him. I had never had such a vision before, so that in itself, seemed miraculous.

As this inner vision unfolded, I found myself overcome with sadness and grief. What I myself would do in the future was not revealed, but I sensed that my faith would also be sorely tested.

The empathic pain I was feeling for this Yogi was nearly over-whelming. I began to weep. I literally felt as if I was dissolving in a cascade of my own tears. I was feeling the pain of his words, of his future wounds, the pain of loss. My heart was breaking with the sadness and grief of the vision he was describing, and that I was envisioning, of each one of these students leaving this magnificent Yogi.

The miraculous experience of having this vision, and the enormous love and compassion it evoked for this powerful and inspiring teacher, drew out of me an urgent inner commitment to serve him, to stand by him through thick and thin. I sensed (it was as though I was shown, or an understanding was transmitted) how painfully I would be tried and tested. I had already been struggling with my own questions about this charismatic teacher and was fearful that I might one day be unable to stand against the logic of my own perceptions versus this new-found faith and commitment, just like the other students in my vision.

So right then and there a spontaneous prayer was evoked … a passionate plea to God for the stamina to withstand whatever challenges might come. I resolved to defy, to override, my rational mind, to disregard my own intuitive voice, to dedicate myself to following this spiritual teacher wherever he might lead me.

The Phyllis House –1969

WITHIN A FEW MONTHS OF MEETING THE YOGI, at his request, I quit my outside job and moved into the little blue Phyllis house he then occupied with a few of his students, and when he asked for it, I even gave him my $10,000 in savings. He began to call me Premka instead of Pamela, as I assumed the role of his primary attendant. In addition to attending on him, I filled in with any letter-writing, transcribed his lectures, and accepted his assignments to re-write the crudely executed translations of various scriptures. I also began to take on more of the responsibility for driving him to his growing number of classes and appointments, as needed.

He made a point of educating the students who lived in his personal household (there were usually five of us) about the necessity for a personal attendant to remain by his side and alert at all hours of the day and night: "You all must understand, sometimes I just leave my body at night when I'm sleeping. If someone is not there to make sure a blanket is covering me, I can just freeze to death. My little dog, Nazee, who is still there in India, is so devoted to me. Once, when I just went out of my body, my blanket slipped off and that little Nazee just grabbed it with her teeth and pulled it back to cover me. Since then, I understood that I must have someone with that much devotion to watch over me when I sleep."

As the Yogi's attendant, my sleeping arrangements amounted to a bedroll I brought out of a closet each night and spread out on top of a carpet on the floor in front of his personal altar and a few

43

feet away from his own bed. His room was one of the two small bedrooms in the little one-bathroom house on Phyllis Street. His own bed was a single-sized mattress, also set directly on the floor. Each night it had become my responsibility to kneel down next to him, massaging him to sleep. He would often pull me into his bed for muffled and secretive sex. Afterwards, though I longed to enjoy lying next to him, hoping to be held by him, he would inevitably nudge me back onto the floor to continue massaging him until he fell asleep.

As painfully disappointing as that was, I accepted his explanation that it was critical that I not fall asleep in his bed, since the other household members would be coming into his room at 4am to begin morning meditation practices. I would dutifully massage him until I heard the rhythmic sound of his breathing. That was my signal that I could finally retire to my own bed. There were also times when I fell asleep slumped over his feet. He would then prod me awake with his foot, reprimanding me later, "Remember Premka, you must remain alert, like a mother with a baby."

One night I woke up and discovered his blanket had indeed slipped away. I quickly reached out to check the surface temperature of his exposed skin. It was icy cold, and I felt panic, fearing that I had failed, and my failure could potentially have been fatal. I re-doubled my efforts to massage him back into his body.

Over the months and years, I learned how to sleep very lightly, to keep my focus on him. For me, he was the most important and precious being on the planet. Devotion, Devotee. There was something so appealing about this concept. As a woman, I had an organic, instinctive urge toward giving myself to a man. In this case, there was the added dimension of serving a higher purpose, surrendering and trusting in the greater wisdom of a superior being. The Yogi seemed to be larger-than-life, so enthralling and engaging. It was reassuring to have a spiritual teacher, someone who had the answers for all of life's ambiguities. If he said something was right, if he confirmed that it was okay, then I need not question any further.

One evening he taught an especially powerful class that got us all high on the vision of an enlightened world in which we all would be the torchbearers. Afterwards, back home for the evening, he shared with the five of us who were living there at that time: "You all must understand that when I teach, I am not the one who is speaking. I actually do not teach, it is just the God who is speaking through me. I am just a channel. That is why I always chant *Ong Namo Guru Dev Namo*[7] before I begin to speak. That mantra just brings in the Divine directly. Then this little 'I' no longer exists. But you must understand that afterwards I am totally drained of all my energy. So now you must just massage me back into my body. "

On this particular night, he had collapsed onto the living room floor of the Phyllis house. Now Ganga, Wallace, Linda, Martha and I began to put our hands on him. Weighing around 200 pounds and measuring 6' 2", there was plenty of him to go around. I was massaging one leg and foot, praying and working hard to bring him back, fearing that he might even be dying, as he would often caution us: "I am not going to live long, you know. I am just a humble messenger, and when I have done my job, then my God will call me back. You should not be sad about it. I am just here for a short time, to remind you of your destiny."

His words would pierce me, and my heart would nearly break at the thought of losing him, ever. That was just about the scariest, most painful thought—the thought of having to go on living without him. As I listened to his words, I dedicated myself anew, silently attempting to mentally, psychically, put all of my life force into him. We all continued massaging while fervently praying.

---

[7] Translation: I bow to the Creator God, I bow to the Divine Guru.

Slowly, I could see that he was coming back around. As his color began to come back, he again spoke, "Premka, you have a special healing touch. I understand that you are the one who will just keep me alive. I am grateful that you have finally understood that you must complete your karmic duty to serve me. That is your only option—to fulfill your highest destiny."

I bowed my head with relief and gratitude. He came back, he didn't die. And I was taking in what he said, feeling special, knowing it was such an honor to have a unique destiny to care for him, to serve him. I understood it was a great privilege, a blessing to be so chosen, to have such a special relationship with such a master.

Along with those thoughts, I felt doors closing all around me. I perceived that I was entering a disciplined confinement, a path of service to him and to the mission he described. And it seemed that, as he often reminded me, I had no choice.

It was nearly a week after my surgery when the doctor deter-mined I was ready to be discharged. True to his promise, Vikram arrived at the hospital to drive me back to the London Ashram. (Surprisingly, there were no bills to pay upon my discharge. Although I was a U.S. citizen, at that time, such medical care in the U.K. was administered for free.)

Vikram was a blue-eyed Brit, just a few years younger than I, with a short and curly reddish-blonde beard and a recently adopted turban wrapped around his prematurely balding head. Before being renamed Vikram Singh by the Yogi, he was known as Vic Briggs and was part of the London music scene, playing lead guitar for Eric Burdon and the Animals, as well as playing in recording studios with such musical greats as Jimi Hendrix and Jerry Garcia of the Grateful Dead.

Now Vikram Singh drove me across a bustling, but wet and dreary London. Parking in front of a small grey, stone building, he helped me out of the car and protectively escorted me down a short flight of cement stairs to a tiny courtyard that served as the entry porch into his basement apartment. The front door opened directly into a nearly empty living-room, about 20 feet square, and mostly situated below ground level, with a few small windows up near the ceiling that let in light and air. The room was brightened by wall-to-wall orange shag carpet and pure white walls. There was a shoe rack by the door and a few cushions stacked neatly along one wall.

Vikram was one of the early wave of students whose attendance at Yogi Bhajan's kundalini yoga classes in L.A. had earned him the designation of 'student-teacher: as trained by Yogi Bhajan'. He, along with several others, had been quickly sent out by the Yogi to other states or other countries, to teach classes and open ashrams. Vikram, who had dual citizenship thanks to his American-born father and British mother, had been sent back to his place of birth in London. He now held weekly classes in this carpeted living room. Those classes were what qualified this small basement apartment to be designated as the London ashram, though no other students lived there.

As I came through the front door, I was immediately comforted by the familiar fragrance of fresh ginger root, cinnamon, cloves and cardamom that had been gently boiling on the stove in the tiny kitchen. This healing combination of spices was the basis for a tea recipe that the Yogi had been sharing over the years, with all of his students. The specific quantities and combination of ingredients had been dictated by him and spread via written recipe to all ashrams and teachers in training, under the affectionate name of 'Yogi Tea'. About eight years later, this recipe was the basis for a multi-million-dollar herbal tea business by the same name.

Directly across the room was a door into the one and only bedroom and its adjoining bathroom. The room had been graciously set aside for my convalescence, while Vikram Singh had set up a makeshift bed for himself on the floor of the living room/yoga room. Still weak and tired from my ordeal, I gratefully crawled in between the white cotton sheets covered by a warm down quilt and fell into a much-needed sleep.

The First Trip to India
1970/71

IT WAS BEFORE DAWN when our 22-hour Air India flight landed at Palim Airport in New Delhi. There were 84 of us traveling with the Yogi and everyone who had access to a window had eager faces pressed against them to try and catch a first glimpse of the much anticipated and mysterious, Mother-India. Though the sky was mostly dark, a wisp of pink was threatening to break through the smoky haze that hovered over this sprawling city. Even from inside the aircraft, I could sense the air held a chill as it was December, the last month of 1970.

The city was just waking up and hundreds of thousands of household servants, inside little cement cubicles that served as kitchens, were lighting small fires for heating up the traditional morning chai (tea). All those fires, many still fueled with dried cow dung, added to the clouds of diesel exhaust that mingled with the dust—dust that was generated by the animal-drawn carts carrying loads of vegetation into the city from the surrounding farmlands.

As the doors of the aircraft opened, I was immediately struck by the smell, the totally unique smell of the land herself, inundated by the centuries of birth, death and decay that formed the dust and filled the air. It was the earthy smell of an ancient land. Not a bad smell, nor a good smell either, but one that was utterly unlike anything else and would, in my sensory memory, forever be identified with India.

Our group of 84 Westerners made its way through all the chaos of Passport Inspection, luggage collection and Customs, while I watched the Yogi from a distance. He was greeting old comrades and former superiors from his prior career as a Customs officer at this very airport. As we moved toward the outside of the building, our ragtag group of mostly white-skinned Americans was a curiosity that drew pressing crowds of unselfconscious onlookers, as well as the inevitable eager beggars.

After what seemed hours, we were boarded onto two hired buses and with all of our luggage piled precariously high on the rooftops, we began to inch our way into the stream of traffic. And what a tumultuous stream it was! We found ourselves riding alongside a wild array of everything from tiny scooters loaded with an entire family of five, to camels wearing blinders and moving as though they were still gracefully plodding across desert sand dunes. Or next to elephants, or odd-looking little black taxi cabs, or bicycle-propelled rickshaws and rickety but colorful flatbed trucks. Every conceivable form of transportation was there, and every pace was unique. Yet amazingly, it all managed to flow along with almost no form of regulation and no apparent rules. Everything and everyone was naturally accommodating one another. And it was noisy! Because every motorized vehicle appeared to be propelled by the sound of its own horn.

As I took it all in, I felt a dissolving sensation, as so many presumptions about the world and about life, were giving way. It was as if I had stepped back in time, back into another century, into another era, onto another plane of existence. Up to this moment I was virtually confined by my own unquestioned beliefs and unchallenged assumptions about life, about the world. Now I felt as if a blindfold was being removed, as I opened to a whole new reality.

I also sensed I had been brought back home, as a deep part of me recognized the spirit of this land. This sensation was totally separate from the visual encounter. My inner soul 'knew' India, even as my conscious mind could barely grasp the external chaos and disparity: the poverty so visible in roadside shacks and shanties, housing that was pieced together out of scraps of tin, cardboard, plastic or fabric, the deformities that the poor had thrust into my face as they begged for money, the makeshift carts and vehicles that carried unimaginably large and precarious-looking loads.

The rational mind, the left-brained requirement for order and organization was being challenged and blown away. At the very same time, some part of me understood, recognized and embraced it all. My heart swelled with gratitude to have found Mother India again. Indian people refer to her this way, as Mother. For me, she also felt like that, like the mother I always longed for. It was as though my soul had been holding its breath, and now I could let it go, I could exhale. I felt that my spirit had found its way back home.

Our buses were headed for the ashram of the Yogi's master, Maharaj Virsa Singh. As we rode along, I looked over at the Yogi. He was sitting on an aisle seat a few rows ahead of mine, riding along in the bus with the rest of us. To my perception, he looked painfully out of place. I felt that he should have been riding in a limousine or carried on a palanquin, not bouncing along in this rickety bus. He was sitting very straight, looking unusually serious and determined, wearing an elegantly tailored, rust-colored woolen coat with a Nehru-style collar, embellished by an ornate jeweled pendant hanging from a 22-carat gold chain. His dress accentuated his innately regal appearance, as did his freshly re-tied white turban and neatly groomed black beard. His head was held particularly high, with one hand holding onto the back of the seat in front of him. He was intently staring out the front window of the bus, as though the very strength of his will was guiding it to its destination.

The plan, from the first inception five months earlier, was that Maharaj Virsa Singh's ashram (named Gobind Sadan) would serve as the base camp for our group's intended three-month visit.

From the time of the Yogi's first arrival in the United States, he had placed a four-foot high, head-to-toe framed photograph of Maharaj Virsa Singh at the center of his personal altar. He bowed before this altar daily as he explained to us, "Maharaj Virsa Singh is the one who has sent me on this mission to the west. Maharaji is not an educated man, but rather he is regarded as a *sant* (saint). His knowledge comes direct from God. He has many prominent people who just come to him for guidance. I have been serving in his ashram for many years, along with my wife." Now that image was about to become flesh.

Our buses eventually pulled up in front of a small compound of adobe-like structures, surrounded by six-foot high mud-brick walls. We all disembarked and were instructed to wait patiently. After a short time, accompanied by a small entourage of his close disciples and advisors, Virsa Singh appeared. He had a slightly darker complexion than the Yogi though he looked to be about the same age, around 40, and also stood about six feet tall. Unlike the Yogi, Virsa Singh had a slender build. His face was well-proportioned, and he probably would have been considered handsome, but his expression remained serious and unwelcoming, his eyes shielded and suspicious.

Virsa Singh was uniquely dressed in layers of impeccable white, starting with a long white shirt (kurta) that reached to his mid-calves and which had characteristic slits up each side. His lower legs were covered by long white stockings. He wore a white turban, softly wrapped around his head. Over the turban he had draped another layer of thin cotton fabric that hung loosely on one side, while the other end lay across one shoulder. All of this immaculate white garb gave him a distinctive appearance, a kind of perfection, an untouched quality—like one might expect of a holy man, of a spiritual teacher. His sandaled feet seemed to barely touch the earth.

Standing alongside him were two women. One of them was Inderjit Kaur, the wife of Yogi Bhajan. For months I had been anxious at the thought of meeting her, uncomfortable about my own relationship with the Yogi. Although I was certain that, as a devotee, I was not a threat to her marriage, still I was very uncomfortable about what this Indian woman suspected and how she might react towards me. The fact that I was now nearly three months pregnant, made that discomfort all the more intense.

This was also the first time the Yogi and his wife had seen each other in about three years. However, she remained standing at the side of Virsa Singh, whom she regarded as her teacher. Between husband and wife there was no joyful greeting, no visible expression. The tension in the air was palpable. Yet, in spite of this cool reception, the Yogi stepped forward with his hands folded in front of him, and reaching down, touched the feet of the man he had called his master.

In the days and weeks leading up to this moment, there had been many instructions to each of us about Indian protocol and customs. Now, putting those instructions into practice, Lehri Singh and I followed our teacher's example, and each one of these fellow travelers and students lined up behind us, to take a turn at bowing and touching the feet of Virsa Singh, while he never changed his distrustful expression and did not appear to be impressed nor happy to see any of us.

Since he didn't speak any English, this awkward reception was concluded when the Yogi spoke up, "Eh Lehri Singh and Premka, please just have everyone gather up their luggages. There are sevadars (servants) who will just help to carry all these bags. They will take you to where you all will be staying." These local sevadars, who did not speak any English, helped unload each bag piled high on top the buses. They then balanced these suitcases on top of their turbaned heads and guided us along dirt pathways to the group's accommodations. These pathways were formed by the elevated borders of now-barren fields and irrigation ditches which created a natural barrier between these ashram buildings and a little tent city.

The tents that had been set up for us were brown, army-issue, secured with stakes and ropes and set on the barren earth. Inside, the Indian-style cots (called charpais), were set out in rows like an army barracks. These were to be the group accommodations! Such Spartan living conditions were not what any of us had expected. Yet surprisingly, no one voiced any major objections or resistance.

Designated with the title of Group Leader, Lehri Singh (aka Larry Wentink) had been serving for the past year as the head of the Ahimsa Ashram in Washington, D.C. He was a young man, in his mid-twenties, about 5'8" tall, with hazel eyes and a short brown beard and mustache and was the only one of the group who was wearing a turban. Lehri was one of the first wave of kundalini yoga teachers who had been sent out from Los Angeles little more than a year earlier. The Yogi called him 'son' and had arranged his marriage to the young, green-eyed hippie girl named Ganga, who was also part of our entourage. Apart from the Yogi, there was no one in this group who had ever been to India. None who spoke the language.

I was given the title of Tour Secretary, which translated as the Yogi's assistant/attendant and the liaison between him and the group. When the Yogi instructed me to put my personal luggage into the room assigned to him and his wife, my hesitation and discomfort were quickly over-ridden by his insistence, "Your job is by my side, Premka. You are my devotee, and I do not want my wife to take that role."

The humble adobe room that the three of us shared allowed for each of us to have our own single-sized bed. Each of these charpais was set against one of the three barren walls. The fourth wall was interrupted by the entry door. There were no closets, so our luggage was pushed beneath each bed. Clotheslines were strung across the corners, useful for hanging or drying clothes.

During those first days, I was busy assisting the members of our group to orient themselves, and in the evenings was often present during tense exchanges between husband and wife. I was amazed at the seemingly endless hours they spent talking in their own dialect. Though it was clear there was great disagreement they never really raised their voices. Bibiji would often cry, and I personally found it painful that there was never any physical contact between the two of them—no hugs, no sitting near one another. Nothing.

When I had a chance to speak with him privately, I questioned, "Sir, aren't you being awfully hard on Bibiji? She's been here waiting for you for nearly three years. She must have felt very alone and abandoned." (Bibiji was not actually her name, rather a term of respect that is traditionally given to women, and this was the designation he had given us for addressing his wife.) It's very painful to see her crying all the time. And it doesn't give a very good impression to your students."

He replied with great determination, "Premka, you must understand, in Indian tradition a wife is expected to keep the faith and trust of her husband, first and foremost. For a wife to put her trust in any other man is a betrayal. It is the highest insult. She never even properly greeted me. And she didn't take care that all of our arrangements were properly made. I was counting on her, and she let all of us down."

Finding these beliefs and customs to be so inflexible, I persisted, "But didn't you both choose to follow Maharaj Virsa Singh? It seems to me that she has been acting as his devotee, like you. And apart from taking care of your children, that has been her life for these three years."

Maintaining his determined stance, he continued, "Premka, she made a choice to stand there with Virsa Singh, instead of her devotion to her husband. This cannot be tolerated, and I can never forgive this. Fate is sealed. You will see that I do not give in. You have not seen this side of me. If I decide to cut off a person, that is it. There is no turning back. My own sister, Parkash, when she betrayed our family—you ask her. I have never forgiven her." I felt tremendous compassion for Bibiji, as I heard his inflexibility, and I prayed I would never make the kind of mistake that would cost me so dearly. The thought of being cut off from him was terrifying.

In the subsequent days, I was nearly always at my teacher's side as we spent hours in meetings, sitting on the thinly carpeted (i.e. cold!) concrete floors, in a semi-circle. Virsa Singh established the apex of this circle and was always accompanied by an entourage that included Indian Army personnel, some business or political men in Nehru-collared suits, and a woman named Nirlep Kaur, who was a Member of the Indian Parliament.

There were also other Sikhs who came from the villages outside of Delhi. Mostly farmers, they wore a style of dress and ornamentation from centuries earlier, from the time of the living Sikh Gurus. They carried antiquated swords and guns, and some wore steel rings that encircled the tops of their turbans. I learned that these steel rings were not just ornamental, but also provided protection to the head during sword battles and served as potential weapons that could be hurled at attackers. These unsmiling and rather fearsome looking villagers stood guard at the ashram's entrance, reminders of another era, and of a warrior lineage that spanned nearly 500 years of Sikh history.

No one bothered to speak any English in my presence, so I was left to intuit what was transpiring as I witnessed any changes in the Yogi's posture, or the intensity and volume of the verbal exchange. Though his demeanor always appeared respectful, even uncharacteristically humble, I could tell by his eye movements that he was busily calculating. As I saw the changing expressions on faces and the rising pitch and tempo of discussions, it was obvious that there were major conflicts between the Yogi and our hosts. Whenever we would be dismissed from a session with Virsa Singh, the Yogi would march away looking serious and generally displeased. Hurrying to catch up with him, I asked, "What happened? What's going on?"

His answers were generally vague, as he kept much to himself, but occasionally he offered some small clues, "I am surprised that this man who I have trusted for all these years seems to be manipulated by politicians. It seems that he is just 'in the pocket' of this Nirlep Kaur. She is a Member of Parliament and he is too much influenced by her. Something is not right."

For the rest of the group, these first days were spent settling in and recuperating from the long travels across more than 12 time zones. During the days, our assigned buses were available, along with translators, to take people out to the bazaars of Delhi. Dollars were exchanged into rupees—and the shopping began. The Yogi encouraged the shopping frenzy, suggesting everyone buy appropriate clothing and head covers for visiting temples, as heads are always covered upon entry to any holy shrine. The women in our group were instructed to cover their legs, to wear long, loose pants for bowing down in front of shrines and for sitting cross-legged on temple floors. Also, we were all encouraged to find inexpensive shoes that could easily be removed before entering temples and private homes. Indian custom regards shoes as 'dirty' and they are never worn indoors.

Soon the invitations from Sikhs throughout Delhi and the Punjab began to pour in—an overwhelming response to photos and newspaper reports of our arrival and the resultant curiosity about this unprecedented group of white Westerners visiting India under the leadership of a Sikh. Indians in general, and Sikhs in particular, are well known for their hospitality, which always includes food and chai. It quickly became apparent that we would be eating wherever we went, and the days and nights were filled by one invitation and one meal after another. In the Indian culture it is considered an insult to refuse to eat, no matter how many times per day food is offered.

In the midst of all of this activity and navigating a foreign culture and language, there was little time to dwell on my personal condition. With barely any warning, one day the Yogi arranged for a private car and driver and the two of us slipped away for some personal 'business' in Delhi. He directed the driver to a small, hole-in-the-wall clinic, leaving me there in the hands of a supposed female doctor, who carried out the abortion, without anesthesia. (It turns out that abortions were also illegal in India, and she was no doctor!) Afterwards, the Yogi returned to pick me up and took me to rest at the home of long-time friends of his, Mr. and Mrs. B.P. Jain. He explained to them that I was having a very painful menstrual cycle, requesting them to allow me to rest for several hours while the Yogi went about his other errands.

It was a few days later, following another very tense meeting with Virsa Singh, when the Yogi took me aside, along with Lehri Singh, "Son, I want you to announce to our group that they are to pack up all of their belongings. We have an invitation to stay at a mango farm, on the other side of Delhi. It will be a better location for us. We will be leaving by noon. Please see that everyone is set and on time."

As soon as there was a moment to speak privately, I inquired about this sudden change in plans and accommodations. The Yogi explained, "You must understand, Premka, I had to make a choice. Virsa Singh was demanding that I turn all of you over to him. Can you imagine? I could not agree to this request. I had to make a choice, I had to take a stand. So I have honored my end of the bargain. That is why I have asked you to be the one to hand over to him the $60,000.00 in our group funds. You are the witness that we have given over these funds which were supposed to be used to build our accommodations. But now we are on our own. It's better this way. It is the Will of the God."

From the beginning of our journey, I had been responsible to carry the Yogi's bag, a kind of pouch made of a soft corduroy fabric. This bag held the Yogi's personal book of daily prayers, a few items such as a fresh, full-sized cotton handkerchief, his wooden comb, his mala (prayer beads), his passport and $60,000 U.S. dollars, in cash.

Throughout the prior months of negotiations via long-distance with Virsa Singh and Bibiji, those funds had been earmarked for construction of lodging facilities for our group. The breakdown in trust between Virsa Singh and the Yogi had been brewing long before our arrival in India. And that breakdown is what had resulted in our group living in makeshift tents, as Virsa Singh awaited physical delivery of the promised dollars.

The announced hour for departure came and went. The legendary lateness of 'Indian time' had become a familiar source of humor amongst everyone. But eventually luggage was loaded and with all present and accounted for (we had developed a buddy system to be sure that no one was inadvertently left behind) we boarded the buses taking us to the next phase of our adventure. This time, the Yogi as well as his wife, traveled in private cars, instead of the buses that transported the rest of us.

The new accommodations had been offered by a wealthy Sikh landowner. He had also provided our transportation and escorted us to his large commercial mango farm in the countryside outside of Delhi. Although the group was still housed in tents, instead of army brown they were colorful red, blue, yellow and green striped, with interior partitions that helped create a semblance of privacy.

Instead of a dusty barren field, they were set in the cool shade of spreading mango trees. (To the delight of some members of the group, these mango trees also provided shelter for some thriving marijuana plants.)

This diverse group of students quickly settled into the new arrangements. Every individual who had chosen to come on this spiritual journey to India had been drawn from yoga classes now being taught around the country. Most had taken kundalini yoga classes with the Yogi himself, and many had participated in Summer Solstice gatherings held in similarly rustic environments in New Mexico. There was a young man named Allen Weiss who was a medical student from Hershey, Pennsylvania; an already grey-haired man named Jim Baker, who owned and managed restaurants in Los Angeles; a family of four who owned a health food store in Marin County, California; the tall red-haired daughter of Congressman Bingham of New York and her blonde and blue-eyed four-year old son, Taiki; as well as my own 18-year old sister, Nina. The ages and backgrounds of everyone was very diverse, ranging from 4-50. There was no common dress code, and most everyone had longish hair while the men all had some degree of facial hair as well. All in all, it was a pretty rag-tag looking group.

The Yogi's wife moved along with us to the mango farm, where the three of us again shared accommodations in the only structure on the property. It was comprised of one large room containing numerous empty charpais, stacked up along one side. I reasoned that it must have been used as a kind of dormitory for the field workers during the mango picking season. The floors and walls were cold adobe or cement, with no glass windows, just some window-sized openings with vertical metal bars. The windows could only be closed for privacy by way of heavy wooden shutters that latched together with crudely fashioned hardware.

I carried on with my duties of taking care of the Yogi's personal needs, his appointments and scheduling. Husband and wife continued to discuss their issues, and Bibiji's face was almost always swollen from crying. He maintained a cool and distant attitude towards her.

For the other members of the group, daily yoga classes and morning practices were organized. Prior to this trip, the thousands of students who had been drawn to Yogi Bhajan really only knew him as 'the Yogi' or as Yogiji. (In the Indian tradition, the 'ji' is added onto a person's name as a sign of respect.) None of us knew much about Sikhism, and most certainly none of us were looking for a religion. In fact, many of us were drawn to yoga as an alternative to the religions in which we had been raised. That was certainly the case for me.

However, now we came to discover, when the Yogi taught his classes, all along he had been speaking of the Sikh Gurus by name, quoting the Sikh scriptures and telling stories of Guru Ram Das and the Golden Temple of Amritsar. This spiritual journey to India turned out to be almost exclusively (apart from a visit to the Taj Mahal) focused around the historical temples and forts established by the Sikhs in northern India. We were hosted in various congregations by wealthy and prominent Sikhs, including the Maharaja of Patiala. Before traveling out from New Delhi, we were also received by Indira Gandhi, the female Prime Minister of India.

Our Group Leader, Lehri Singh, managed to quickly pick up a few key phrases in Punjabi and was soon able to express our gratitude, our great respect and appreciation in Punjabi, his voice booming out over the antiquated microphones that were placed before him at receptions and Gurdwaras[8]. We provided such an

---

[8]   The word used as designation for a Sikh temple. Literally translates as the 'Dwelling place of the Guru'.

unexpected novelty for these Indians, to see our white skin, our blue eyes, to hear us speaking greetings in their local dialect. After so many decades of British rule, where they had been treated as second-class citizens in their own land, they could hardly have imagined white Westerners embracing their language, their traditions, and their religion. And now the Yogi who had inspired all of this, who was clearly and most visibly a Sikh[9], was suddenly being elevated to rock-star status throughout the Sikh world.

The culmination of our travels brought us finally to Amritsar, to the Golden Temple. We were eagerly welcomed as the guests of the SGPC (the administrative body for the Sikh religion) and provided with accommodations in their guest house situated across the street from the temple entrance. By this time, we had been temple-hopping for about two months and had learned much of the protocol required when visiting Gurdwaras.

As soon as we arrived in Amritsar, I witnessed the Yogi become utterly one-pointed in his urgency to touch the dust, reach the threshold of his beloved Guru's house. Those of us who could keep up with him, were practically running as he seemed to barely touch the ground in his rush. I followed his lead as he took a sip from the tank surrounding the temple, as he bowed and made offerings at various shrines along the parkarma (walkway), and as he bowed his head at the threshold of the temple itself and finally to make his prayers and offerings before the Guru, the Sikh holy book. I saw and felt his tears—of relief, of joy, of gratitude.

After nearly two full months of traveling throughout the Punjab, everyone gratefully settled into the Nanak Niwas rest-house accommodations for the remaining weeks before we were to return

---

[9] Sikhs were and still are, a minority religious sect of India. Sikhs primarily occupied the northern agricultural lands of Punjab and are distinguished by the wearing of turbans and beards for the men. The Sikh religion is distinct from either Islam or Hinduism.

to the U.S. Many began a routine of early morning (3am or 4am) dips in the icy cold tank of water surrounding the temple, before sitting through the morning prayers and kirtan inside the temple.

For me, those precious early morning hours, the Amrit Vela[10], were totally rich and deeply nourishing to my soul. It was an exclusive time inside the temple, free of crowds, requiring no pushing or shoving to get in. (Although it is a principle tenet of the Sikh religion to rise in the hours before the sun rises, most Indian Sikhs do not come to the temple at such an hour.) Once inside, each of us sought out our favorite spots, some climbing up marble stairs to the golden-domed rooftop, or securing a private alcove quietly tucked away on the second floor.

The continuous recitation of the words of the Sikh Gurus is one of the powerful features of the Golden Temple. At the same time as the prayers are read in various locations throughout the Temple, some of these prayers are being sung by dedicated musicians. Such devotional activity builds an amazing vibration. This is the gift of this temple. It is powerful to be in the presence of this much enthusiastic prayer. The music is so rich, with the Eastern scale and raga system being so intricate and emotive. I found so much identification and mystery in it, which was partly due to the fact the scriptures were being sung in a language I did not understand. I could only feel it, sense the deep current of love and devotion for God. The rhythm of the accordion-like harmonium accompanied by the two tabla drums, combined with the resonant voices of the devotional male singers, was deep and soulful. I felt I could listen to it forever.

In fact, I had been listening to it for a few years now. In his own room back in L.A. the Yogi had reel-to-reel tape recordings that he requested me to play for him, in the mornings and before

---

[10] Literally: The time of nectar. The 2-1/2 hours before the rise of the sun.

going to sleep at night. They were tape recordings of the kirtan music performed by some of these same musicians.

For these nearly three months, we were immersed in a totally foreign culture. So by now we were accustomed to following instructions, going places without knowing where we were, and doing things without really knowing why. So it was that on one of the final days before our departure, we were instructed by the Yogi to join him early in the morning to participate in a special ceremony. Once we had gathered, the Yogi led us from our guesthouse accommodations, to take the now-familiar barefoot walk on the freezing cold marble floors that formed the walkway encircling the Golden Temple.

On this particular morning, instead of crossing the walking bridge to the Golden Temple itself, without explanation he guided us to another building, directly across from the Temple's entrance. I was merely following his lead, and now the two of us stood at the small entrance at the bottom of a precariously steep and incredibly narrow staircase, as he directed each of these students of his to climb to the top of those stairs. Once everyone had begun their ascent, he signaled for me to also go ahead up those stairs.

Now I became rather alarmed! As his devotee, as his attendant, over the years it had been my practice to walk behind my teacher, opening doors for him. This was unusual, this was different! He was holding the door for me, directing me to go before him. I obeyed but felt even more dismayed as the door closed behind me ... and he did not follow.

I sensed then that this was a major shift, that this teacher of mine was turning me over to the Guru of the Sikhs. I feared this change almost as much as I embraced it. I had fallen deeply in love with the sound current, with the language and rhythms, with the all-embracing definition of the 'One God of all creation' that the

Sikh scriptures describe. Nonetheless, change is by definition full of uncertainty.

Once inside the room at the top of those stairs, we were received by five men in turbans and tunics, their lower legs and feet bare. After arranging us into a circle surrounding a giant steel bowl, they began reciting prayers in the language of the scriptures. At the same time, they used large, double-sided swords to stir water while dissolving sugar wafers in the bowl. The scraping of the steel sword against the side of the steel bowl generated a rhythmic sound that accompanied their recitations. It was hypnotic.

From beyond that room, we could also hear the morning kirtan from the Golden Temple blaring over the ancient loudspeakers, and the smells of incense and cooking fires filled the air. All of us stood in a circle, surrounding the bowl, with our hands pressed together in a prayerful pose, as instructed.

The recitation of prayers in the Gurmukhi[11] language seemed to go on for hours, the rhythmic stirring, the hypnotic music, the chanting and recitation. Then, when all the five prayers were complete, the five men took handfuls of the sugary water they had been stirring, and instructing us not to blink, they threw it into our eyes! Shock! Another round and more was dripped onto the crowns of our heads, and finally we were told to pass the bowl around, to drink all the remainder of that mantra-infused sugar-water.

It was hours later when we emerged, dripping with the sugary ceremonial waters, cold and hungry. Without truly comprehending the significance or import of what had taken place, we had just received the highest Sikh baptism, called Amrit.

Stepping out onto the exterior walkway, we were immediately surrounded by Indian Sikhs who were enthusiastically handing

---

[11] The original language of the scriptures, which utilizes the same phonetic alphabet as the spoken language known as Punjabi.

us all sorts of gifts and paraphernalia, including small knives called kirpans, and the holsters for holding and wearing them. We received shawls and turban fabric, the prayer beads, called malas, wooden combs. So many things, and though all of them were speaking in a language we didn't comprehend, it was clear that they were congratulating us as we were being herded along to the langar (the traditional communal free kitchen of the Sikhs), to be served hot chai, and some vegetable-stuffed prantas[12]. And a 'group snap' had to be taken. I was vastly relieved when I finally spotted the Yogi on the outer edges of the crowd.

I was contemplating all of it, sensing from the moment the Yogi had directed me up those stairs that he had turned me over to the Guru of the Sikhs. I knew that it was a very significant and important shift. I felt some sadness as well, because that seemed to mean that the dynamic of our relationship must have changed. I feared something was not as it had been. Right along with the sadness, there was exhilaration, excitement at having a Guru that had the validation of hundreds of years of tradition.

I awoke from my first refreshing nap after leaving Hillingdon Hospital, to the sounds of Vikram practicing on his harmonium. An accomplished musician already, Vikram was naturally drawn to understanding the subtle and complex rhythms and scales of the Eastern raga system. Although it was comforting for me to hear these familiar sounds, I was also feeling an anxiety that I struggled to keep at bay. Although my rational mind understood the logic and the necessity for the Yogi to leave me behind while he returned to the United States, I experienced once again that emotions are

---

[12] Also called a 'stuffed chapatti', this tortilla-like flat bread is filled with vegetables and spices.

seldom appeased by logic. My own core wound of feeling unwanted and unloved was easily triggered, so the present circumstances provided a perfect set-up.

With one huge concern on my mind, I finally found the courage to ask the Yogi, on one of our costly and therefore brief and infrequent international long-distance calls, "Sir, who is taking care of you while I'm away?"

His voice traveled across the telephone wires with a lilt, 'Ah, not to worry, Premka, you must just get yourself well. Remember Susan, who came to India with us? She has come to Los Angeles to take my care while you are just getting better. She has come all the way from Miami. She is a 'bull' you know. She is a Taurus and she is very strong. You are delicate, and we need to take good care of you when you come back. We all are just praying for you to get better and come soon. Here, you can just say 'Sat Nam' to her. She is learning to wear good clothes and tie up her hairs. It's all working out. You need not worry for me."

This news hit me hard. My greatest fear was manifesting. Smashed, crushed, heart-broken, it appeared that I had been replaced. He already had another woman there, doing the one job that I assumed would be exclusively mine, forever.

The Yogi had often told me, "Premka, you and I have a karmic relationship from many lifetimes. But you must remember that I am just living three lifetimes in this one lifetime, and I have to do many unusual things. Although it is not in your destiny to get married, I understand that you still need this kind of physical relationship. I am just fulfilling an obligation to you because of past karma. I have no need of any sexual relationship. I am beyond all of that."

There was another story he loved to tell me, "In a past life, you were a Temple Priestess in Burma, and I was a celibate monk in that temple. The Temple Priestess is also the ruler of the country, and she does not take a husband because she is the Sovereign. Rather she just chooses any man whenever she wants to have sex. You used to taunt me and try to make me to break my vows of celibacy. In this lifetime, I am just settling this past karma."

What a strange concept. It was painfully confusing. I would plead with him: "But sir, I really am fine without sex. I would really prefer to be celibate. I don't want to have this conflict and confusion. I always feel torn because you're my teacher and you have a wife, and you're teaching everyone to be either celibate or married. I would really prefer to just serve you as a devotee."

I desperately wanted to be free of the torment, of the duality of our relationship. It seemed to me that life would be so much simpler, so much more pure and perfect if it didn't have this confusing complication. These conversations always ended in his laughing at me, rocking his head from side to side, Indian style, saying, "Na, na, you cannot live without it, I know that."

Was that really true, I wondered?

Finally, after nearly ten days of recovery in London, I was flying back to Los Angeles. The constant droning hum of the jet engines drowned out every other sound as my flight headed toward home, leaving me free to reflect on the twists and turns of my life and to wonder about what changes might be coming.

As eager as I was to get back to L.A., my insecurity and anxiety were equally as strong as I wondered: *Would I still be taking personal care of Yogi Bhajan?*

That was the big question on my mind. Although I had pleaded for celibacy many times, my issues of abandonment and rejection were more gripping than my independent moral conviction. More than anything, I wanted to continue to have my personal access to him, to be the 'special one'.

Besides, I had given him the power to guide my choices and my actions. My life had been turned over to him. At his request, I had given up my outside job and moved from my own apartment to a bedroll on the floor of his room. I had sold or donated all of my possessions, including my car.

Surrender was the goal—in exchange for enlightenment? I actually didn't presume that I could achieve enlightenment. It seemed to me that enlightenment was something reserved for Jesus or Buddha ... or this teacher of mine. Rather, I had entered into a teacher/student relationship—a kind of bargain—where I sought to fully surrender my ego, my personal preferences, my dualistic mind, to the superior wisdom of this teacher from India who proclaimed himself to be an enlightened spiritual guide.

Much of what our Yogi taught centered around the practice of surrender, the transformational power of devotion, the necessity to subjugate to the Will of God and thus to overcome ego: "Spiritual teacher is God's own representative. The relationship between teacher and student is elevated, because teacher is the instrument for practicing surrender to the Divine. Surrender to the teacher is never a surrender to the man—it is only symbolic—a practice to learn how to do the real surrender to God's Will."

Being in love with Yogi Bhajan was completely contradictory and confusing, because he was so much more than just an ordinary man to me ... and to his thousands of followers. Like the first time he touched my breast, sex with him seemed almost clinical, impersonal, lacking in real warmth or passion.

I kept hoping to feel held or loved or embraced or wanted. Instead, I was always left feeling more confused. He often told me: "You must understand, Premka, that I am not having any sexual relationship with anyone. If that is what you think, then you are badly mistaken. I have no need for sex. Sex is just an urge, like the urge to urinate."

Which still left me wondering: *If I'm feeling so much duality about it, then why does he insist, against my pleas to the contrary? Is he truly God's channel? Is he really above the rules? Is our relationship sanctioned by God? Who decides what God sanctions? What is our relationship really about? Does he love me in any personal sense of the word?* These questions and doubts haunted me in spite of his reassurances.

When I missed my period a few months earlier, I was incredulous. Though I had been in a short two-year marriage, I had never before been pregnant. With the Yogi, I had counted heavily on the rhythm method and divine protection. Birth control pills were a rather new development and still experimental. I had used them for a time during my marriage, but then medical issues kept me from continuing.

When the Yogi initiated sex with me, I assumed that he was infallible, that he either had God-like powers or was, at the very least, divinely protected. I naively assumed my status as his devotee, along with careful timing, would serve as adequate contraception. This magical thinking of mine was ripe for a large dose of reality.

When I told him about my missed menstrual cycle, the Yogi was quick to advise me that, 'We will have to get it cleared out, Premka, not to worry."

But I quickly jumped to another hopeful possibility as I blurted out, "But sir, it must be God's Will! Couldn't I just be sent to some secret location where I could raise this child? This must be a very special being and I really want to have this baby."

The Yogi was unmoved, "That will not work out, Premka. There is no need to be emotional. Remember what I have taught, that the soul does not enter the womb until the 120th day of pregnancy. Meanwhile, I'll make arrangements to take care of whole thing.

You just keep relaxed. We are planning a trip to India, and I have the right connections there. After all, I worked for many years in Interpol and as a Customs Officer. Once we reach Delhi, I know the right doctor for our purposes."

His admonishment confirmed what I already feared, that I would never be allowed to keep this child. Although painfully disappointed, I was not surprised. Since abortions were still illegal in the United States, it was somewhat reassuring to know that he had a plan. His unwavering clarity always seemed to clear my own head and heart. His confidence and his self-assured manner were such a contrast to my own fluctuating and tentative stance in life. He always had answers. In fact, it was his self-mastery, his power-filled approach to every situation that made him so appealing to me.

Over the past few years I had heard him share this particular teaching with his students—stating that there is a time, at the 120th day after conception, when a growing fetus becomes infused with the ineffable quality of soul. This is the moment when an individual consciousness enters the fetus that has been developing inside the mother's womb.

He even instructed the women of our community in how to create a ceremony, a circle, that was to be held on the 120th day of a woman's pregnancy. The mother-to-be was to sit in the center, while other members of the community would join in prayer, chanting and singing, to call in the soul of her child.

As with so many things he taught, this interpretation made perfect sense to me, because it seemed to align with the biological/medical reality, that up until the end of that fourth month is when most miscarriages occur and when abortions can be safely performed. I accepted this teaching of his as another confirmation of the perfect order within the universe, the perfection of the Creator's design.

The Stuff of Legend

A S I HEARD THE INSTRUCTION TO FASTEN SEATBELTS, and noted the sensation of the flight beginning its descent for our landing in Los Angeles, I wondered what changes might have occurred in my absence? On our last telephone conversation from London, the Yogi told me he had a surprise for me. I was still puzzling over what that might be. As I walked up the ramp into the receiving lounge at LAX, I watched for the young man who had come to meet me, one of the Yogi's faithful students he had named Baba Singh. In India, Baba is often used as a title of respect, usually applied to elders, those who have ascended to some degree of spiritual wisdom.

Far from elderly, Baba Singh was only about 25 years old, but he carried his name and the role of devotee with dedication, with an almost comical, exaggerated seriousness. He received me with eyes averted, bowing his turbaned head, folding his hands, respectful yet studiously impersonal. Baba's complexion was very fair, while his beard was nearly black. He had big, guileless dark brown eyes and a prominent nose.

I was feeling shy and self-conscious, unsure of what to expect, wondering what he knew, what people knew or thought about my time in London. I had confidence that the Yogi could expertly orchestrate conversations, so everyone was distracted from talking about anything so personal. In this regard, Baba Singh carried out his role perfectly. As we drove back toward home, he made small talk, about the Yogi's growing class attendance, about the great blessing of having such an amazing spiritual teacher. He never once inquired into what had happened to me, about why I had been hospitalized in London. *So what did the Yogi tell him?*

Within 30 minutes, we pulled up in front of the little blue house on Phyllis Street. Baba Singh came around and opened my car door. Extending his hand to help me out, he encouraged me, "You go on ahead, Premka. The Yogi is waiting for you. I'll bring your luggage inside."

Excited and relieved to finally be home, I practically ran past the tiny patch of grass that served as a front yard, and up the concrete steps. Letting myself in through the front door, I immediately heard the Yogi call out from the next room, "Premka, is it you? Come, come quickly."

It only required a few strides to cross the sparsely furnished living room and to find the Yogi sitting on the full-sized bed in the spare bedroom. He was leaning with his back against the wall, his legs outstretched. Crowded into the 12 x 12 room with him were a few of his closest students, some sitting cross-legged on the floor, a few of his other female household members seated on the far end of the bed. He appeared to be in a light-hearted and relaxed mood, with his long hair hanging down, and his house turban loosely wrapped on top of his head, in a comical way that seemed to make him more approachable. His large size, his radiance, his physical beauty and his powerful projection were nonetheless awe-inspiring.

Though I wanted more than anything to rush into his arms, I dutifully assumed a respectful demeanor, my palms together, head bowed, truly grateful to see him, to be here and to be alive. I had been on an emotional roller coaster ride since that blood-soaked landing in London. To finally hear his deep, loving and reassuring voice and to see him sitting there as though nothing had changed, nothing was different, was already a huge relief.

Unexpectedly, he reached out with his strong arms and those beautiful, graceful hands that I loved, pulling me to him, into his big chest, his soft round belly. My whole being relaxed into him. Fear, tension, anxiety, all melting away in this fatherly embrace. This was what I had been longing for, to be safely held in his powerful and loving arms. There I was, in the only place I wanted to be... ever. Feeling his strength, held by him, home at last. I relished it for those few moments, while everyone looked on. I heard the telltale sounds of a few sniffles here and there, as the onlookers were impacted by the love between us.

Breaking the spell of this emotional moment, the Yogi firmly pushed me back into an upright position as he reached over and pulled something out from beneath the pillow next to him and announced, "Here it is, Premka, I told you I would get it done. Now I have kept my promise."

Incredulous, I opened my hands to receive it—a dark blue, hard-bound book, with the title 'Peace Lagoon' written across it in golden ink. There it was, a published book—the American-English rendering of the Sikh daily prayers, with my name, Premka Kaur, on the title page. I had worked for many months on refining the translations of these prayers and hymns of Guru Nanak and the other Sikh Gurus. I did not have a grasp of the original Gurmukhi language in which they were written, so I didn't technically translate them. Rather, I had worked from various English translations that had been written by Indian scholars who had used an antiquated British-style English.

It was the Yogi who selected which of the hundreds of translated prayers he wanted me to render into more flowing American English. I had accepted the assignments as part of my own spiritual practice, something I presumed the Yogi was using to keep my mind absorbed in holy thoughts. Obediently, whenever the Yogi was out of town, I had locked myself away, for hours and days at a time, attempting to discern the message of each line, of each word, and then to express that message in poetic rhyme and meter.

Now, that dedicated sadhana of mine had been published as a book of prayers that would become a source of inspiration and guidance for our young and growing community. My recent days of fear and uncertainty in London were being washed away by the glow of this moment. What an amazing surprise, what a great welcome home.

As I continued to sit there next to him, I now looked around to see who else was in the room. Shakti was there, and she seemed genuinely happy to see me, exuding a new level of love and respect. Black Krishna was also there, and I soon learned that the two of us were being exalted as heroines, as the Yogi began to share a story from our adventures in India: "When I saw for myself that Virsa Singh just expected that these students who came to India with me must now touch his feet, I knew this was not right. Then, when he even demanded that all those students who came with me should be handed over to him, this I could not agree. So finally we packed up and left that ashram. But Virsa Singh has some wealthy and prominent disciples and main one is Nirlep Kaur. Nirlep is a Member of Parliament. I know her from many years, and I know how corrupt she is. Well, she became jealous and angry when we all separated from Virsa Singh, so she sent her henchmen, her gunmen, to just shoot me."

As we heard him tell this story, it brought more tears around that little room, and I saw them also welling up in Black Krishna's eyes, as he continued, "When they just showed up at that one gathering, carrying those rifles, Premka and Krishna just threw themselves on me. They pushed me onto the ground, and they became the human shields, to protect me. I can never forget this. I am learning from them what is a real devotion."

His words were imbued with prophetic power and respect.

And what had been for Krishna and me a natural and automatic response, to protect our teacher in a potentially life-threatening situation, seemed elevated in his re-telling, to the realm of myth: a story about devotion, about the quality and dedication of a devotee and the profound love for one's spiritual teacher.

As I sat there and listened, I sensed an inner re-organization. Very subtly, I sat up a little straighter, my head lifting a bit higher. I also sensed the hint of a new weight upon my shoulders.

He continued, "I have told you all that I am not important. I am just an instrument to guide you to your destiny to serve the humanity. I just share with you what God channels through me. Otherwise, can you believe that any man can know this much? I don't think so. It's not me, it's just the Divine that uses me for His purposes." I marveled at the way he held everyone in rapt attention, each person within hearing range hanging on his every word.

"You know, sometimes I just request Shakti to play for me the recordings of my own lectures, and I'm surprised my own self. I can't even believe those words came out from my mouth. Do not misunderstand me, I am not the one who is speaking. I'm just a humble servant. That is my Virgo nature. Rather, it is the God working through me. I'm just preparing you to become the examples of how to live as pure humans, as God intended. I'm grateful that you are just answering the call. What we're creating is family. You're learning to be there for each other. That's what a family does."

Dressed in a sleeveless white t-shirt, a brown light-weight woolen shawl draped around him, with his turban askew, his delivery transported us and transformed him. There was a palpable sensation that seemed to emanate from his being. It wrapped us all in a cocoon of inclusion, a kind of 'pink love' that held us and bound us together.

I was barely breathing, not wanting to break the spell. Taking it all in, I gathered information through all of my senses. I caught the telltale aroma of the sandalwood incense burning on the altar, mixed with the fragrance of ginger, cinnamon and cloves from the steaming hot yogi tea that Martha was quietly serving to everyone. The sound of Gurbani kirtan was playing on the reel-to-reel tape recorder in the other room—music that now brought up new memories. I had heard this music for more than two years without really knowing its source. Now it carried new impressions from seeing the live musicians, the various bearded and turbaned ragis (musicians) we heard playing in dozens of Sikh temples throughout India. And the words they were singing were the Gurmukhi words that had been rendered into American English in this newly printed volume I now held in my hands.

It all felt surreal. Nobody in this room knew what I had been through. They didn't know that I had been pregnant, that I had an abortion in India. They didn't know I had nearly hemorrhaged my life away, while keeping that secret. Or how alone and how afraid I had been. That was all held in a compartment of my inner world, a backdrop of my mind, while this more delicious drama played out in front of me. A drama with a much more appealing script, as the Yogi began to share another anecdote, "I have seen this Premka sitting in the garage, with a blanket wrapped around her legs and feet to keep from freezing, while she worked long hours just typing those pages of scripture, or preparing the letters I asked her to write. That blanket must be saved for the archives, that afghan which she has used. We are creating a history, and world will just marvel at this history one day. You will see."

It was a lot to let in. His delivery was dramatic and spellbinding as he transformed simple events into epic proportions. I was surprised and amazed at the stories he told and felt myself disappearing into them. As I witnessed it all, I sensed that Premka was becoming the stuff of legend.

In the months and years that followed, I found myself moving along with the whirlwind of change that spun out around the amazingly energetic and endlessly creative Yogi. The community of souls that was drawn to this charismatic teacher, and then gathered around us, was a welcome replacement for my own family-of-origin. Those who were the most inspired by his teachings became kundalini yoga teachers and set up ashrams and yoga centers, opening them in nearly every major western city of the U.S. and also Canada, Mexico and Europe and then as far east as Japan.

Under the Yogi's guidance, this community quickly evolved from new agers and hippies to yogis and seekers, and then to Sikhs. At the core, we were passionate idealists, dedicated to living a yogic lifestyle, vegetarian and health-conscious, with a newly evolving devotion to a simple concept of a Creator God that seemed more personal, and less dogmatic than the religions of our parents. Most of this baby-boomer generation had been turned off by religions claiming special status or exclusive access to the Divine. Instead, almost en mass, the youth culture of my generation had turned to Eastern philosophies, systems of yoga and meditation.

From the very first yoga classes with Yogi Bhajan we were unknowingly being inspired by his interpretations of the Sikh religion. When he taught the yoga classes that drew us to him, he didn't just teach exercises and postures, he was sharing a whole philosophy.

In addition to an all-inclusive Creator God, his words and his teachings not only validated long hair, and flowing beards, they virtually institutionalized them. The Yogi explained: "This is the Creator's design—the human is created with these long hairs on top of the head. Think of it—no other creature has this. These hairs were put there for a purpose, they are actually the antennas. They draw in the universal energy."

Heads would nod, eyes would shine with excitement at the significance of these words! We had a special purpose, a special mission, and we were eager to share these ideas with all who would listen. And so we did.

The Yogi would continue, "God never made anything without a purpose. You can just see it, that all hairs grow to a certain length only. Whenever you cut these hairs, or you shave them off, it requires energy to grow them again. When we don't cut them, we preserve that energy which is needed for the higher consciousness. You must understand that it is only God who grows these hairs. It is the ego of the man that interferes with God's own design. We are the ones who have taken the vow that 'As the God has created us, so we shall be.' That is our commitment as Sikhs of the Guru, as the pure ones, as Khalsa[13]."

He also made a cosmic yet very personal connection for us, saying, "This is the time when the Aquarian Age is dawning for the whole humanity, and you are the special ones who felt the call to just let the hairs grow. This was your natural instinct. Nobody taught you this. Simply you were ready, time was ready, stars were lined up. It is the sign that you are the children of the Age of Aquarius. You are destined to lead the humanity to live as God has made us. That is the foundation of our way of life, and that is what we will bring to the world. You are destined to be the teachers of the coming New Age."

Our Yogi was part of a wave of teachers from the east, including Rajneesh (Osho), Swami Satchidananda, Swami Mukhtananda, Maharishi Mahesh Yogi, to name just a few. Each of these Eastern teachers seemed to be called to the west by this generation of

---

[13] Khalsa: Pure One. The title given to baptized Sikhs

youths who were seeking gurus and spiritual teachings that could awaken and enlighten. The Yogi pursued and inspired a camaraderie between all of these new age leaders as well as the heads of more traditional religions, inspiring festivals such as the 'Holy Man Jam' in Boulder, Colorado. He spoke and offered the dedication prayers for major pop festivals. He saw the connection between the youth and their music and its alignment with their spiritual pursuit.

The Yogi gave words and structure to what we were feeling— an urge to discover and even to exemplify a viable alternative to the prevailing materialistic and militaristic Western culture. This sense of mission, of a larger purpose, along with our lifestyle practices of yoga, meditation and vegetarianism, this larger-than-life Yogi and an inclusive perception of ourselves as a huge extended family—these were the primary unifying principles of life in our community.

Yogi Bhajan was the catalyst for each step of our formal transformations as individuals and as a community. He had also made changes in his own appearance over the years: from wearing western-style pants and shirts with brightly colored turbans, to churidars and kurtas and finally to his trademark floor-length white robes and white turbans. He had shifted from being called 'the Yogi' to elaborate titles like 'Siri Singh Sahib' a title meant to designate him as the Chief Religious and Administrative Authority for the Sikhs of the Western Hemisphere.

At one time or another, every young or newly inspired Sikh turned to Yogi Bhajan as a wise and guiding spiritual teacher and father-figure, to find him or her a wife or husband, to help straighten out a marriage, to learn how to discipline a child, or to solve employment and financial issues.

For those of us in the inner circle, life around Yogi Bhajan was never dull, always filled with the unexpected, as he turned lives upside down in order to get them back on track, as he would inspire a new business venture, direct an engagement or arrange an on-the-spot marriage.

Monogamy is a strict religious tenet for a baptized Sikh, and thus marriage served as a means to insulate his youthful followers from straying into sexual liaisons. He was quick to match up any single men or women newly entering the fold. He would relocate people in the blink of an eye and 'family' businesses multiplied and grew to employ the newly turbaned Sikhs as they moved to or from Los Angeles, New Mexico, New York, Canada, Europe or even India or Japan.

Thanks to all of this relocation, by the middle of the 1970s, the 3HO community in Los Angeles (dubbed the International Headquarters) had grown to a residential population of nearly 500 students, mostly all being housed on or around Preuss Road. The summer headquarters in Espanola, New Mexico, was nearly as large. There were family businesses that ranged from vegetarian restaurants named Golden Temple Conscious Cookery, to Yogi Tea, Sunshine Oils, the Sunshine Brass Bed Factory, Golden Temple Grains, Wha Guru Chews, Kettle Chips and Akal[14] Security.

Businesses were blooming everywhere, couples were being matched up sight-unseen and it all seemed to proliferate as if by magic, or by God's Will, as the Yogi would say. He himself appeared to have super-human energy and to be guided by prophetic insight. As busy as he was, he sought to remain accessible and available to all of his students and teachers on a nearly non-stop basis, sleeping only three to four hours per night.

As I had feared, my function and status elevated me beyond the role of personal attendant, though I still traveled as part of his entourage throughout Europe, Japan, Asia and North America. I

---

[14]   Akal: Undying

was in attendance for private audiences with two popes, received the Dalai Lama in L.A. and met Prince Charles at the Los Angeles World Affairs Council. I was also leading small groups to India or meeting world leaders or religious leaders on behalf of our organization.

Being at his side through all of this growth and transformation, I knew individuals before they became couples and then, in a sense, I met many of their children even before they were born. I felt great affection for these students, and a personal concern for their families. My own contacts with people in the community were less social, rather they were defined by my role, by my administrative functions and ever-evolving titles which came to include Secretary General, Administrative Director, Editor of Beads of Truth and author of Peace Lagoon. The Yogi continued to publicly repeat stories of my heroism or my sacrifices or my prowess as a meditator as well as stressing the unique power of my prayer. I found myself being elevated and emulated.

As a consequence, much of my outer demeanor was conditioned by what I perceived as the expectations placed upon me. There was virtually no opportunity to be true to myself because there was no encouragement to know who and what my own self was. Instead, I was very focused on being true to the image that was repeatedly defined for me.

My own strongest inclinations included my great desire to please along with my need to be wanted, to be loved. At the very same time as all of this outer façade was being constructed, and I was being loaded up with responsibilities for overseeing offices and accounts, for organizing events and editing a quarterly magazine, I found myself more and more in a working relationship with the Yogi.

And a woman spoke, saying,
Tell us of Pain.
And he said:
Your pain is the breaking of the
shell that encloses your understanding.
Even as the stone of the fruit must break,
that its heart may stand in the sun,
So must you know pain.

~ KAHLIL GIBRAN

My Little Girl

MEANWHILE, MY OWN BIOLOGICAL CLOCK was ticking as I moved into my 30s. My mothering instinct was also being stirred through an exceptionally personal connection I felt with a little blonde girl named Nav Jiwan Kaur.

We made our first deep contact when she was only an infant. I was standing in line one Sunday morning in Espanola, waiting for my turn to bow down in front of the Sikh scriptures. A tiny blonde-haired girl was facing towards me as she was being carried over her father's shoulder. Nav Jiwan gently and deliberately reached out her tiny hand and took hold of my extended finger, while she seemed to look deep into me, with an exceptionally calm demeanor, an acceptance of life that deeply touched me. She also had a delicate beauty that appealed to my aesthetic sense.

As the years passed, during the summers when I was in New Mexico, I continued to find myself drawn to Nav Jiwan. It was a mutual attraction. By the time she was about four years old, she would regularly find her way onto my lap for some part of the two- and three-hour morning services at the Sikh Gurdwara in Espanola.

She was a delicate little girl with hair so fine that many of the strands around her face never achieved any length before they just broke off in disarray. Most, but certainly not all, of those scraggly wisps of hair were wrapped up inside an often disheveled-looking turban. Sadly, one of her eyes wandered, giving her a cross-eyed gaze. Her eyes were otherwise a deep blue, observant, absorbent and clear.

It tugged at my heart to see that this adorable little girl was often dressed in clothes that were wrinkled and worn looking. Her thick and homely eyeglasses were often smudged, and the unattractive frames might be bent or broken.

Looking back, I can see that Nav Jiwan was unconsciously touching a lonely and unacknowledged little girl who lived inside of me. And the mother part of me wanted to step up and take care of her.

One late summer day in 1980, as everyone was socializing after morning sadhana, I had an opportunity to sit with her father, Guru Tej Singh. I took the opportunity to make an offer that I had been contemplating, "You know, Guru Tej, I'd really love to do something special for Nav Jiwan. Do you think it would be alright if I had a few outfits made for her? I have some designs in mind that would look really cute on her." For years now, I had used a local seamstress in L.A. custom designing my own dress-length kurtas to wear over the Indian-made pants (churidars).

His response was immediate and enthusiastic, "Wow, I think that would be awesome. Nav Jiwan really loves you, you know. She's so lucky to have Premka as her auntie."

I had an extensive collection of fabrics that I had gathered throughout all of my travels. Now I was excited at the prospect of having clothes made for Nav Jiwan, of transforming her into a real-life little princess. I continued, "It would be so much fun for me. Do you think her mother would be okay about it? I don't want her to feel that I'm interfering in any way."

Guru Tej quickly assured me, "Oh, I think she would be happy for Nav Jiwan. Anyway, I'll let her know about your offer and I'll make sure that it's all right with her."

It was a few days later, following the Sunday morning services in Espanola, when the Yogi called me aside. That morning Nav Jiwan had been sitting beside me during much of the service. Like most

Sikh children, she was very disciplined throughout the long hours of prayers and chanting. But now the Yogi found it necessary to reprimand me, "You must understand, Premka, you have a special role to play, and it does not look good if you have some favoritism going on with this Nav Jiwan."

I was totally surprised at his criticism. I believed I had found a safe place to express some normal human affection. Defensively, I responded, "Favoritism? But, sir, she's just a child. What is the problem if I'm having a relationship with a little six-year old girl?"

He had pulled me apart from the rest of his security and entourage, his right arm outstretched in a way that afforded a kind of private space for us, as his hand rested on my left shoulder. Overriding my objections, he continued, "Premka, you must understand that I'm just building your image. As Secretary General you must remain aloof and above personalities. This is the requirement of the one who sits on the throne. It is a lonely job, no doubt, but that is what it is. I have always told you this."

He **had** told me this... many times. I had never quite resigned myself to the idea and I wasn't at all willing to give up this minimal human contact, this tiny expression of my own feminine nature. *What could be more natural and innocent?* So I protested, "But sir, I think it's good for people to see me caring for a little child. I think it shows my humanity, my compassion, that I'm looking out for people in our community, that I care about them. What could be wrong with that?"

He continued, "I'm just telling you that it can be misunderstood, and people will feel that you are biased and you have favorites. As the Siri Singh Sahib, I must have equal compassion for all of my students. Isn't that true?"

I tried to reply with some equanimity, "Yes sir, and I feel that I do have equal compassion for everyone. I just want to help one little girl who has some special needs. I can agree to be less personal in public, but I would actually like to help her to get proper medical attention for her eyes. And, I want to have a few things made for her so that she has some attractive clothes to wear."

"I understand, Premka. Just remember that emotional involvement is to be avoided. You are the Secretary General for entire congregation—not just this one little blonde girl."

In the course of this exchange, I felt my simmering resentment toward the Yogi. I already felt isolated, and more and more distant from him. He was occupied, busy with an expanding organization of students that had grown to over one hundred thirty centers world-wide and he traveled to one center or another virtually every weekend. His entire nuclear family had also come to live in L.A., and his daughter and two sons plus his wife, Bibiji, all required his attention. He also kept adding more and more staff members (women) around him. Each one was given a special administrative function to fulfill, along with titles and offices, as a huge organization was proliferating.

Yet there was a hidden side to all of it. These new staff members were also drawn into a personal relationship with him. For years I had suspected there was more to these relationships than met the eye. And the truth was that I resented it. I resented being replaced. I resented the lies that he told me for years—the years of denial—a denial that affected my core relationship with my own intuition, my own knowing.

I was having a very hard time with the test of 'covering' my teacher. He had often repeated a story, meant to illustrate the purity of devotion expected from a devotee: "Your devotion must be so pure, like that devotee who can just walk in on her teacher. Finding him naked and having intercourse with one of his female students, her response was to put a blanket over both of them, and quietly leave the room, closing the door behind her. That is the sign of a pure devotion. To see but not see."

I beat up on myself for seeing what I saw. Caught up in duality and conflict over what I knew was happening versus his claims to the contrary, it was difficult for me to sort out my own appropriate response.

Now his challenge to my innocent affection for a child was pushing me up against a wall of irresistible resistance. I explained to him, "The experience of loving and caring for this little angel child seems to me to be a safe and natural outlet for my own personal emotional expression. I resent that you seem determined to give me no such option. You are, after all, designing this entire community and all the rules we live by. So why can't you write this story so that I get to have a loving friendship and parenting experience with a little child? What could be so wrong? What would it take away from you? Or from anyone? Instead, you are insisting on isolating me, while you deny yourself nothing. Why are the rules different for you than for me, or for anyone?"

He clicked his tongue and shook his head from side to side, in an expression that implied that I was being way, way out of line, "Premka, you are just forgetting that I am your spiritual teacher. You are comparing yourself, and this is the wrong attitude for a devotee. Don't you realize that you are the example that people look to? You should just remember that your photograph is on people's altar. That is a big responsibility, and you must live up to it."

As always, he had the last word, and I gave up in exasperation. The role, the responsibility of my office, of my titles, of being Premka, always took precedence.

As the summer months in Espanola came to an end, along with all the other staff members, I shifted my office and residence back to Los Angeles. Once there, I went ahead and began making phone calls, contacting some of the medical doctors in our L.A. community, getting referrals and gathering information that confirmed that there were medical techniques that could potentially correct

Nav Jiwan's wandering eye.

In spite of the Yogi's admonition, I went ahead and began to arrange for her to make a trip to Los Angeles. I pleaded my case, "Sir, I just want to do whatever little I can do to help Nav Jiwan. I have learned that her eyes might be corrected if she received the right care while she is still so young, and I want to bring her here for an examination. I've arranged for her to stay overnight across the street from the Estate, with Dr. Saram and Kulwant. That should satisfy the issue of looking too personally involved." Although he scowled, he didn't stop me from going ahead with my plans.

Four city blocks comprised the length of Preuss Road., and by this time in 1980 the street was conspicuously occupied by the turban-wearing members of our community. New yoga students and seekers came to take advantage of the opportunity to attend classes regularly taught by Yogi Bhajan. On class nights or on Sunday mornings, the sidewalks held a steady stream of white-turbaned, and flowing chuni-draped Sikhs decked out in their brightest and finest white, walking to or from the Sunday services or nightly classes held at Guru Ram Das Ashram.

Wherever a house was owned by community members or dedicated to communal living arrangements, Yogi Bhajan would give that house a name, designating it as an ashram. Then a sign would be created, depicting the new official name of the house. The Yogi used the names and titles of the Sikh Gurus to teach, to inspire respect, even reverence. If a house was named after Guru Arjun Dev, there would be stories shared about the life and historical contributions of that particular Guru. Then those stories were handed down and would be shared by all who came to live in that ashram.

Early morning hours throughout the community were always dedicated to the practice of yoga, chanting, prayer, singing of hymn-like songs. Many other English songs were original creations and contained a mixture of Gurmukhi and English lyrics.

In front of the house in which I lived, there was a white sign with royal blue letters that read: GURU RAM DAS ESTATE. It was installed on the flagpole in the front yard. (The entire neighborhood was humble lower-middle-class residential, and yards were small, so the designation as an Estate was verging on absurdity.)

On the morning that I was to drive her to her first doctor appointment, I brought Nav Jiwan to the Estate to share some breakfast and some hot yogi tea. I also took the opportunity to dress her up in one of the new outfits I had made for her. I wrapped a beautiful, neat white turban on her head, and draped a fresh white chuni[15] around it. She looked so amazing—her delicate features so beautifully framed in all that white. Photographing her with the portrait lens on my Nikon camera, I experimented with shooting her in profile, which allowed me to capture her image without a hint of that wandering eye. My camera feasted on her innocent beauty, on her sweetness, her exuberance, her spontaneity, while she was having fun posing, with having so much attention. I was delighting in her playfulness, her childishness and her joy.

A double-car garage with attached bathroom and laundry room, was located at the rear of Guru Ram Das Estate. While maintaining the outward appearance of a garage, the interior had been fully renovated and decorated to serve as a guest accommodation, while it also currently served as my personal quarters. (Almost everything the Yogi owned or designed had more than one function, with the result that nothing could ever be personally claimed by any of us who served him. We could claim no ownership, hence no attachments. Theoretically, no ego—a primary goal of our spiritual path.)

Everything in this suite of rooms was white! White walls,

---

15 A filmy scarf of silk or a silk-cotton blend.

yellowish white carpet. White upholstered couches and chairs. Bright, immaculate, and very white! The main room was spacious and open, with high ceilings crisscrossed with white painted scissor trusses. White closet doors, white dressers, a big brass bed (painted white) and a white painted steel ladder that led up to a loft. Yogi Bhajan said, "Living in a space that is totally white is a meditation in itself."

Feeling a need to establish some coziness within that huge room, I had set up my personal meditation altar and sleeping space in the low-ceilinged loft. This loft had once been an attic, used only for storage. Now, like the rest of the quarters, it was nicely finished, painted white and fully carpeted.

Sleeping directly on the floor was a yogic practice the Yogi advocated to all of his students. We were instructed to sleep flat on our backs for maximum spinal health. (The teachings of Yogi Bhajan addressed virtually every activity of daily life, including sleeping.) This specific minimalist practice achieved a practical dual function, since bedrolls could be put out of sight each morning, leaving a room open and meditative.

In the time we had remaining before we needed to drive to the doctor, Nav Jiwan and I were crawling around in my sleeping loft as she helped me to fold and put away my bedding from the night before. We were thoroughly enjoying the unique experience of spending one-on-one time together, and I was even feeling a little giddy, excited for the outcome I hoped was coming for Nav Jiwan. I was also feeling more playful than I had felt in a long time.

Unexpectedly, I was struck by the absurdity of the two of us crawling on all-fours. As that thought entered, we were at the same level, Nav Jiwan and I. Our eyes met as we faced each other, on all fours—and we both burst out laughing!

We laughed, and we laughed harder, rolling with laughter on that thick white carpet. I laughed until my sides ached, until tears were streaming down my cheeks.

There were no words spoken between us, just deep and cathartic laughter. It seemed to me that we both got some cosmic joke, and in that instant, there was no separation, no age gap between us. All roles and protocols had dropped away. We were looking into the mirror of one another and witnessing some level of the truth of Being. How amazing that I was sharing such an expanded cosmic moment with a six-year old child! Oh my God, it felt so good to laugh like that. What a release! What a relief! Yet along with the relief I felt a familiar twinge of sadness for how rare it was...to experience such spontaneity, to feel seen and to connect at such a deep level with another being, and to really, really laugh.

Gradually Nav Jiwan and I pulled ourselves together and made our way down the ladder to our scheduled appointment. The doctor confirmed what I had hoped, that Nav Jiwan's eyes could be strengthened and even straightened. She was given new prescription eyeglasses, new eye exercises and new hope before flying back to re-join her parents in Espanola.

New Mexico had become the summer headquarters of the Secretariat staff, and at the end of May that following year, I traveled back to The Ranch in Espanola. By mid-June more than a thousand members of our international community would be flying or driving across the country, to attend our big yearly events: Summer Solstice celebrations, the Women's Training Camp and the Khalsa Children's Camp.

Summer was a very busy time in Espanola and usually included an influx of Indian VIPs who came to see what had become a phenomenon—the 'American Sikhs'. And the Yogi loved to impress them with the comparatively lavish accommodations he had created in America. All of that activity amounted to lots of responsibilities for me, for all of the staff, with lots of protocol to be observed.

On a personal level, (of which I was supposed to have none) I looked forward to seeing Nav Jiwan again. The clothes I had made for her the year before were already beginning to look wrinkled and worn, and her turban always needed some skillful adjustments, so whenever possible I would discretely tuck in those mischievous blonde hairs. She assured me that she was keeping up with her eye exercises, which could potentially even improve her vision. In the meantime, she wore her newly prescribed glasses which were slightly more flattering than her old ones.

Nav Jiwan was seven years old that year, and when she came and sat near me during the morning services, she sat up straight and tall. I was gratified to see her beauty shining through.

It was still early in that summer of 1981, when I received an urgent phone call, on my private phone on the ranch property. It was Wha Guru Singh calling and I could hear the dread in his voice, as he urged me, "Sat Nam, Sardarni ji. You need to come to the Espanola Hospital right away. Nav Jiwan has taken a fall. She was out at Nambe, on an outing with the other children. Please come quickly."

I gasped with fear, "Oh my God, is she alright?"

The mind can barely grasp it. One minute someone is there, so alive, so vibrant. The next instant the life force departs from the body.

And it's so final. The mind rebels, the heart cries out to God to retract that which is so unthinkable ... and yet no amount of prayer or disbelief can change it. Death is such a final and intractable thing.

That little angel child had stepped off the edge of a trail and had fallen down the side of the mountain. The single supervising adult scrambled down to her, lifting her frail body from the rocky bed of the dry stream. She carried her all the way back to the parking area and drove her the ten miles to the Espanola hospital.

There were no cell phones in 1981. Even if there were, it wouldn't have made a difference. Nav Jiwan had landed on huge boulders and her tiny, beautiful and fragile skull, had been crushed.

So many layers of grief, of pain, of loss—for her family, for the community and for me. Additionally, I could hardly escape questioning whether her death was some kind of punishment designed especially for me. Within the context of that time in my life, I was inclined to perceive a direct link between external events and the Will of an all-powerful God. Was I being punished for my personal attachment...or for my opposition to my teacher?

*A human being is a part of the whole
called by us "universe", a part limited
in time and space. He experiences
himself, his thoughts and feelings
as something separated from the
rest, a kind of optical delusion of his
consciousness. The striving to free
oneself from this delusion is the one
issue of true religion. Not to nourish it,
but to try to overcome it is the way to
reach the attainable measure of peace
of mind.*

~ ALBERT EINSTEIN

Entering the
World of Politics

THE GROWTH AND EXPANSION OF THE COMMUNITY and the mini empire being generated continued unabated. My heart had been broken at the loss of Nav Jiwan. The Yogi knew this and his way of dealing with such intense loss was to push me to get busy with life. I had multiple responsibilities, projects and events to keep me occupied and moving forward.

There were travel assignments several times each year, and these transitions to other countries and circumstances brought a sense of relief from the relentless activity of my self-critical mind as well as allowing a break from the tedium of work and responsibilities in L.A.

One year, when the political tensions between the Yogi and various high-ranking Sikhs of India had been particularly heated, the Yogi sent me to India on his behalf. He explained to me that the political climate was so volatile that year that his life was under threat if he were to go himself.

On this particular visit, the Yogi directed me to hold press conferences in which I defended the adherence of the Western Sikhs to the stricter standards of the Sikh teachings and practices, as well as the Yogi's adoption of titles and authority over the Sikhs of the Western Hemisphere.

(His claim of the title of Siri Singh Sahib of the Western Hemisphere was a huge point of contention within various Indian Sikh communities and organizations. They challenged that authority and that claim. They also challenged his own adherence to Sikh principles. From their viewpoint, he appeared to be functioning as a guru to his followers. The Sikh faith strictly prohibits any person from adopting a position of guru.)

I was also instructed to arrange a private audience with Indira Gandhi, to carry a message of our solidarity as a Western body of Sikhs under the guidance of Yogi Bhajan. This message was further intended to convey our community's political relevance on the international political scene. We were putting Indira Gandhi on notice that we were a force to be reckoned with.

News stories covering these events and meetings began to appear in the Indian press, accompanied by my photographs: a white-complexioned Western female dressed all in white with a chuni-draped white turban and the title of Secretary General of the Sikh Dharma of the Western Hemisphere.

Soon, word reached back to the Yogi that my life was now in danger. I received his urgent phone call: "Premka, I have learned that your life is now being threatened. You must return back immediately to America. Gurcharn Singh, Journalist, is making your flight arrangements and will just get you safely to the airport. You must pack up quickly and just come back home."

The idea that my life was threatened felt surreal to me, yet I was flattered and reassured about the Yogi's love and concern for me, and about his reach and his power. He played politics on a level that was far beyond my personal comprehension.

As he requested, arrangements were made, and I was soon boarded on an Air India flight headed for home. As was typical, my flight was scheduled for a refueling stop at Heathrow Airport in London. Over the many years of travel to India, this Transit Lounge had become a familiar place to me and now that I had safely escaped out of India, I was looking forward to one of my favorite indulgences—a freshly baked scone with clotted cream!

As I was passing my time in that Transit Lounge at Heathrow, I arrived at the bottom of a ramp that led up to a mezzanine level. Suddenly, at the top of that ramp, about 60 feet away from where I was standing, I was incredulous to see a tall turbaned man in a floor-length white robe and flowing black beard, surrounded by an entourage of his white-clad followers—the Yogi!

We actually spotted one another at the same instant. Soundlessly and instinctively we each began to run toward one another. The emotion of relief and love was so encompassing that I perceived us moving toward each other in slow-motion, while the moment itself seemed to be suspended and timeless.

Because my departure arrangements had been made so hastily, neither of us had been informed of the travel routes and timings of one another. It turned out that the Yogi was transiting through on his way to teach his White Tantric Yoga courses in Europe. Somehow God/destiny brought us into that time and space, together for a moment of deep relief, love and connection.

Many years later I happened to recall that event in a conversation with Sat Nam Singh, one of the students traveling with the Yogi that day in the Transit Lounge of Heathrow Airport. He shared his own experience of watching the Yogi and me as we ran towards one another. He told me that he saw the entire event happening in slow motion, and that it appeared to him as though our feet did not even touch the ground!

Meanwhile, the political outreach of the Yogi was being developed along with every other facet of the organization. These connections he cultivated became significant as he worked to gain recognition for Sikhs worldwide. Significantly, he had his own lawyers (entitled Chancellors) working on achieving proper recognition and dispensation for the religious requirement of Sikhs to maintain beards, hair and turbans while serving in the military. Over the years he was consistent in donating to both the Republican and Democratic political parties.

In 1977, the year that Jimmy Carter was to assume the presidency, Black Krishna and I were the representatives the Yogi sent to the inauguration event on the Mall in Washington, D.C. It was a cold and sunny morning, as we stood in the crowd in front of the new president-elect as he was sworn in. Afterwards, we made our way to the Lincoln Memorial where we connected with Coretta King, the wife of slain civil rights leader, Dr. Martin Luther King Jr. No introductions seemed to be required as our head-to-toe white garb and elegant turbans and chunis were clearly signifying a religious affiliation. We all took photographs together on the steps leading up to that revered monument.

On one of our yearly trips to India, we attended the Independence Day Parade in New Delhi. The Yogi and a few of us had passes into the VIP viewing area and I was pleasantly surprised to find myself standing alongside Jaqueline Kennedy and her handsome son, John Kennedy, Jr.

PART II

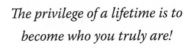

The privilege of a lifetime is to become who you truly are!

~ C.G. JUNG

Snapping in Singapore

IT WAS THE PROVERBIAL FINAL STRAW FOR ME —that one little added insult that upset a delicate and precarious emotional balance. I was savoring a few quiet moments with Yogi Bhajan— one of those increasingly rare times when we were alone in the same room, undistracted by some member of his family, or his staff, or a student, or a VIP of some sort. Over the years I had come to have less and less one-on-one time with him, and this tiny window of opportunity, as Bibiji left the room carrying his empty water glass and before anyone else entered, felt momentarily intimate and personal, like in the early years. I was starved for some personal attention from him, some acknowledgment, some signal, that would reaffirm the personal dimension of our relationship. It was the end of 1982 and Yogi Bhajan and I were guiding a group of over 30 of his students on what had become a yearly spiritual trek to India. Leaving the larger group behind in Amritsar, the Yogi with this hand-picked entourage had split off on a side-trip to visit the Indian Sikh congregations in Singapore, Malaysia and Burma.

Without even looking up from the newspaper he was reading, though I hadn't uttered a word, he zeroed in on my neediness. He was, after all, highly attuned to all the women who surrounded him: "Premka, you are forgetting to be in gratitude. You know you would be just nobody today if I had not picked you up."

Like a cat, every hair on my body seemed to stand on end. My pride, my pain, my 14 years of service to him and the mission, my personal sacrifice, all felt diminished, trashed and insulted by this cruel and dismissive remark.

It wasn't the first time he had said such things. It wasn't the first time he claimed credit for anything of value about me or my life. Actually, he often claimed that kind of ownership over his staff and students. But on this evening, under the heightened energy of a full moon in December, something inside of me snapped and I hissed at him through clenched teeth: "That does it. I've had it. I'm done!"

Propelled by my seething anger, I now stomped out, heading into my adjoining room, leaving the Yogi to absorb my uncharacteristic reaction to his unwelcome criticism. Some slumbering, yet familiar part of me was rising up and silently screamed, "I don't deserve this—I'm not going to take it anymore!"

Within seconds, he followed to find me sitting upright on my narrow single bed, with my arms wrapped tightly around my knees. I was bracing myself against a rage that felt dangerously capable of blowing my whole world apart.

At the far end of my room, he struck a deliberately unperturbed and casual pose in front of the only window in this humble two-star hotel. He had, intentionally or not, selected a strategic location which offered him some dramatic backlighting. He stood, with one foot perched on a chair, elbow leaning onto his bent knee, his long hair hanging loose, while his familiar brown shawl was wrapped around his extensive girth, with one end of it draped over his shoulder.

In addition to being a giant of a man, especially by Indian standards, he was strikingly handsome, and his waist-length black hair and long black beard added to his charisma and exotic glamour. So did his dark and flashing eyes. He had the body of an aging athlete, with the muscular legs of a football player and the extended belly of a man who now spent much of his working life in a vibrating recliner chair with a telephone receiver pressed to his ear.

Nonetheless, his pose was aesthetically compelling and was

surely intended to add to his persuasiveness. With a slightly taunting smile, he began "Ah, my Secretary General, just cool it down. I was only poking at you. You should not be taking offense. You must not forget that you and I have a mission to carry. I don't think that I can live that much longer. You must be ready to handle all of this family we have gathered."

I was in no mood to be flattered into compliance, and through clenched jaws I seethed, "I don't **want** to 'handle things'! Besides, I have no interest in carrying on your mission. I don't agree with the way you run peoples' lives, making decisions for them. I would never be willing to do that and I want no part of it! I mean it. I'm done."

Maintaining his unperturbed demeanor, he straightened up to his full six-foot-two-inch height, and bringing his other foot back to the floor, he continued "Na, na, Premka, you must just have a glass of water and cool it down. Blood sugar must be falling." He walked across the room and, opening the adjoining door wider, he called out into the next room, "Hey, Sat Simran, I need some water here and some piece of fruit for Premka. We need to take care of the Secretary General. She is a very important person, and we need to be sure she gets her food in the proper timing."

Feeling the fire of my anger, and free from any other witness, I repeated to him, "I mean it, I'm done. I don't deserve to be talked to that way, and I will not be part of your staff. I'm going to have my own life. I <u>will</u> get married and I <u>will</u> lead a normal householder's life, like any other Sikh."

Just as I finished my last sentence, Sat Simran appeared, dutifully carrying a glass of water. I tried to conceal any obvious signs of anger in her presence, as my years of conditioning took hold. After all, it was the antithesis of our spiritual beliefs to even feel anger, much less to display it. On this day I had really crossed a line by unleashing some of my pent-up and virtually unacknowledged resentment onto my spiritual teacher. Still, I wasn't prepared to demean myself by exposing that shameful anger in front of another staff member.

"Eh, Sat Simran, just bring Premka one date and a few pistachios. That will lift the blood sugar right away. Then just go and ring up for samosas[16] and pakoras[17], and garam chai[18]. That is what we need—hot food and chai to balance out from too much stress, too much travel. I think we all are too much exhausted."

I remained silent, relieved that he wasn't exposing me in front of Sat Simran, that he was covering for me, creating a distraction and providing me with an alibi. In his subtle way he was letting me off the hook. That's what I had come to expect from him.

I had often witnessed his verbal assaults on Bibiji, or Sat Simran or Soorya—they were his usual whipping posts. I was always offended by that behavior of his, and when I had private conversations with him, challenging those harsh and angry tirades, he would dismiss it as his way of teaching them. But he virtually never used those insulting, prodding tactics on me. On this night we both had crossed into new territory with one another.

Nonetheless, as other members of his entourage began to drift into my room, my sword of righteous indignation had been withdrawn, back in its sheath ... for now. My body and mind were still vibrating with the energy that had been ignited. Composure—I retreated to the familiar place of graceful composure, as the room began to fill with food and people and conversation.

Remaining quietly seated on my bed, I watched the scene unfolding in front of me. I allowed myself to be 'cooled back down' as he put it, soothed and embraced by the rhythms of the Punjabi-mixed-with-English banter, the laughter and the smell of hot chai and steaming hot vegetables that had been deep-fried in a spicy batter.

---

[16] Samosa: mashed potatoes and vegetables wrapped in a pastry dough and deep fried
[17] Pakora: deep fried, batter-dipped vegetable
[18] Garam chai: hot tea

This had become my world, this unseemly blend of cultures, foods and languages. Incense drifted in from the adjoining room, sometimes overcoming the pungent smells wafting up from the teeming streets below: smells of diesel exhaust mixed with fresh animal excrement and the ripe fruits and vegetables of the open-air markets of this East Indian section of Singapore.

Music was playing on a tape recorder in the background: the divine, inspiring Gurbani Kirtan, with tabla and harmonium accompanying the devotional, musical recitation of the Sikh scriptures. The rhythms, the sounds, the smells, the tastes... all of them weaving a subtle and seductive atmosphere.

The blaze of my anger settled down to a more manageable level, more like smoldering coals. But something very tangible had shifted in me, and the inner search was on—the search for my way out.

The next day we departed as planned for the next congregation on our itinerary. We didn't speak about that incident again and Yogi Bhajan didn't appear to worry about it either. After all, he knew that my whole life was invested in this community, in this family, and he probably knew better than I did that I really had no other options or resources. My own birth-family ties had long been strained or were virtually non-existent. After 14 years as his devotee and a Sikh, I no longer had any active friendships outside of this community.

Also, the Yogi often repeated his cultural beliefs about the prospects for a mature woman, "Once a woman has reached 30 years of age, she has reached her peak. From there on, it is all downhill." I was fast approaching 40, so that seemed to be another deterrent, as his every word was received as truth, like scientific fact, and such words formed the teachings that were the ground of the entire community's belief systems.

Added to this picture was the fact that, within this community that had become my whole world, he had crafted a glorified image for me, complete with grand titles and slightly exaggerated stories that exalted me into a legend—a dramatic and highly effective compensation for my own deep sense of unworthiness. Within this insular world of white-clad, turbaned Western Sikhs, I had come to represent an ideal image of a Sikh woman. My style of dress, the specific way I wrapped my turban, my devotion and reverence for all aspects of the Sikh faith, plus my handling of the administration of our growing non-profit organizations, my authorship of books, scriptural translations, all added up to an image that my little sister would sarcastically call 'Pretty, pink, perfect Premka.'

I did take my responsibilities very seriously. The expectation that I must someday take on the leadership of the entire organization weighed heavily on me. Plus, the way Yogi Bhajan defined it for me, my position included the requirement that I relinquish any personal life. His demeaning and dismissive words this night, had touched a really raw nerve.

I was now considering, ever more seriously, the fact that I had been in service to this larger-than-life Yogi for the prime years of my adulthood. I had never been paid a salary for the 14-hour days and 7-day work weeks. (In recent years our CPA had insisted that all staff members be paid a stipend of $300 per month). Instead, I was publicly exalted and given titles that accompanied an ever-growing list of organizational duties and responsibilities.

This latest insult from him brought up all the pain I had endured as I was pushed out of my role as his personal attendant. Private moments and conversations with him were replaced by meetings about organizational structures, new enterprises, budgets and schedules.

In attempting to address the emotional needs of his proliferating all-female staff, the Yogi loved to remind us about the great
benefits we all enjoyed, "You all wear the finest silks. You travel
the world and have private audiences with popes, presidents and
prime ministers. You ride in limousines and drive Mercedes Benz.
You collect the finest fabrics from Europe and even you get your
underwear from France. What more you can want?"

When I had a moment alone with him, I would answer that
rhetorical question, by pouring out my frustration, "I'll tell you
what more I can want—I want to have a life! The Sikh religion is
defined as a householder religion. In fact, it's a basic premise of the
Sikh religion, to live a normal householder's life. You teach that we
worship through work, through devotion to family, not by living a
life of celibacy and self-denial. You are married, AND you have a
dozen other relationships. Why must I be denied even one?"

The truth is that I felt isolated, overworked, over-burdened and
my faith in my teacher was being seriously tested. My own father
used to say, 'The boss may not always be right, but the boss is always
boss.' I resented that concept, and I liked his other favorite quote
even less: 'Do as I say, not as I do.' Those hypocritical statements
embodied the philosophy that fueled my angry rebellion against
my own parents, and now it seemed to be repeating in this alter-
nate-family dynamic.

The odor of hypocrisy was beginning to permeate my view
of my spiritual teacher. Over the years, it had become part of my
administrative responsibility to set the budgets and supervise the
accounts of the three non-profit corporations Yogi Bhajan and his
lawyers had created, and thus to participate in the establishing of
a small for-profit corporate empire that had grown to include Yogi
Tea, Sunshine Oils, Golden Temple Grains and Akal Security. Yet
I personally had no money, and absolutely no assets of my own.

The clothes on my back. That was it. It was the same for all of his 12 staff members ... and all of his staff members were women.

I was becoming painfully aware of all the ways in which I was bound. His off-handed remark in that hotel room in Singapore had set off a chain reaction in me. He had revealed a surprisingly dismissive attitude, and I wasn't going to be lulled back into complacency. I couldn't make a move overnight, but I was determined to find a way. As our side journey drew to a close, Yogi Bhajan and I, along with the others in our party returned to New Delhi.

Siri Brahma Singh was the American Sikh student-teacher who had been left in charge of the other Western students participating in this year's India yatra. While our smaller entourage had been visiting other Sikh congregations, the larger group had been busy with life around the Golden Temple at Amritsar. Their days involved rising around 4am, wrapping up in woolen blankets and crossing the narrow and always busy street to take a cold dip in the frigid waters of the expansive pool surrounding the Golden Temple, finally sitting inside the temple itself for early morning prayers and kirtan.

Upon our return to New Delhi, we were booked into the five-star hotel, the Taj Mahal, and Siri Brahma was there to receive us. He was a devotional and radiant young man, with a warm smile and twinkling eyes. He had a disciplined and respectful demeanor, always assuming a protective and serviceful stance around the Yogi and his staff members.

In recent years, in addition to his martial arts training, Siri Brahma had been studying various systems of healing bodywork. I was looking forward to receiving a Jin Shin treatment after all of the stress of our travels, so as soon as he appeared, I took the opportunity to request him, "Ji, whenever you have time, I wonder if you could come up to my room to give me a treatment? My low back and sciatica are quite painful, and I would really appreciate it if you could come as soon as possible."

In addition to providing security and escort to me and other staff members, Siri Brahma had become one of the only men ever permitted to provide Yogi Bhajan's staff with foot massage, Jin Shin treatments and spinal adjustments. His face lit up with a big smile as he assured me "Yes, I will come as soon as I get Yogiji's luggage up to his room."

When that 'snap' had occurred in Singapore, I had thought of Siri Brahma. There had been many times over the years when I had thought of Siri Brahma.

Do your best
Until you know better
Then when you know better
Do better.

~ MAYA ANGELOU

An Egoless Male?

IT WAS NEARLY SEVEN YEARS EARLIER, in 1976, that Yogi Bhajan had called me from Hawaii, saying, "Eh Premka, I am just now bringing a young man back to L.A. He will be a great asset to you and your staff. I have named him Siri Brahma. You will be surprised to know, he was the personal attendant to Maharishi, and he lived for nearly eight years as a celibate monk! Can you believe it, after eight years of serving him, Maharishi just threw him away?"

Well, that was a first, to attract a former disciple of Maharishi Mahesh Yogi, the founder of TM aka Transcendental Meditation! His next words interrupted my contemplation, "You know, Premka, I am always grateful that Maharishi prepared the way for me by teaching Americans the difference between yoga and yogurt."

This was one of his favorite and oft-repeated comments, so I quickly proceeded to ask a question of my own, "Yes sir, I know, but why did Maharishi 'throw him away'?"

Without hesitation, he answered "Oh, these swamis, they just do that, you know. They keep you close-in for a while, then they push you out on your own. It is a 'sink or swim' trip. He was the in-charge of the T.M. center on Oahu. He came to my Tantric course in terrible pain, so I am bringing him along with me, so he can just be with the family. You will see, he will be very useful to you. He is very devoted, and he will be a good security for me."

The wheels were turning—intuition, imagination, rational deduction or my own desperation? If this man had spent eight years with Maharishi, then he had been with him for as long as I had been with the Yogi, so we must be close to the same age. If the Yogi was bringing him to our headquarters, then he must be very special. Special, as in devotional, disciplined, trustworthy... egoless?

Men were never brought into the staff or the household of Yogi Bhajan: "The male ego can never tolerate another male ego." This statement had been the Yogi's oft-repeated explanation for the predominance of females he kept around himself. An egoless male would be a very unique experience indeed.

That conversation was my first introduction to Siri Brahma. Sight unseen, I had already begun considering how he might fit into my life.

By that time, the staff and household size had grown to about ten American women, plus Bibiji, Yogi Bhajan's wife. We all lived in four different houses along Preuss Road, in the heart of Los Angeles. All of us, except Bibiji, worked at the Secretariat offices and whatever personal lives we had revolved around the Yogi. We ate together, we went to movies together, we attended events together. But there was little opportunity or incentive to develop real friendships or relationships with one another since the Yogi always held center stage. Rather it was more of an emotional roller-coaster ride full of insecurities, mistrust and competition for the Yogi's attention. I periodically felt desperate to get off the ride.

A few days after that long-distance telephone conversation, I drove the cream-colored Mercedes Cabriolet to the airport to receive the Yogi on his returning flight from Honolulu. I observed that the young man who appeared alongside him was wearing a nicely shaped fresh white turban. I surmised that it must have been tied for him by someone at the Honolulu ashram, since tying a proper turban takes lots of practice. The freshly grown reddish whiskers that were sprouting around his shy and tentative smile created a less-than-glamorous appearance.

Looking past that scruffy beard, I observed clear blue eyes, a man of medium height with nicely proportioned shoulders. Most of all I noticed how he kept his eyes averted, head respectfully bowed, as he seemed to be holding back a slightly amused and radiant smile. He had the tentative and disciplined demeanor of a devotee. Self-effacing.

LAX was much more lax in those days (pun intended!) and we were able to park our lineup of white and silver Mercedes along the curbside of the baggage claim area. Each of those cars and drivers had different reasons to be there, either to transport the Yogi's luggage or to follow behind him with his personal security guards, or just to carry other staff or family members. Some of the greeters were in a habit to touch the Yogi's feet, others just to put hands together with heads bowed in reverence. Although he traveled in and out of L.A. nearly every week, his return was always treated with fairly elaborate protocol.

Yogi Bhajan stood outside the receiving gate for a while, leaning with his forearm onto one of Siri Brahma's shoulders, as he greeted the welcoming entourage and gave his report of the Honolulu trip: "The family in Hawaii is growing stronger and more beautiful each visit, and we had a good attendance for the Tantric Course—about 60 students. And, oh my goodness, we ate so much mangos! Those Hawaii guys are in so much love with me—they just brought me cases of the most juicy mangos and we ate mangos every day. We practically did a mango fast! You know you should always take milk with mangos, that helps to cool it down. Otherwise, mango is a very hot food. In our luggage, we have just now brought a whole case of mangos, so everyone can have them in smoothies."

Siri Ram Singh was one of the men in the waiting entourage, and he called out a question, "How was the weather for you, sir? Did you get any time in the ocean?"

"Ah, it was perfect weather, and we just sat in the ocean to clear out from jet-lag. That is the best remedy for all this travel, you know, just sitting in the saltwater, close to the shore with water up to the shoulders, for about one hour at least. I even gave a kundalini yoga class in the ocean, with breath-of-fire. Saltwater just pulls out all the exhaustion, you know. Wonderful!"

I thoughtfully watched all of this typical reception, with all attention focused on Yogi Bhajan. He never introduced Siri Brahma, just kept leaning on his shoulder, while Siri Brahma smiled shyly, sheepishly.

I was honestly considering what this young man could mean to me. I already knew that I wanted a way out of the immediate vicinity of Yogi Bhajan. I was having a hard time reconciling Yogi Bhajan's status as my spiritual teacher and my growing objections to what sometimes looked like hypocrisy and manipulation. At the same time, I was battling another internal voice that criticized me for my doubting mind, for my flawed devotion. The battle was ongoing, relentless and paralyzing.

Luggage was loaded into the waiting cars as the Yogi and Sat Simran climbed into the back seat of the Cabriolet. I looked back through the rear-view mirror as Siri Brahma was led to the security escort car. He turned and watched as we pulled away from the curb. Most likely he was watching the Yogi depart. Still, my feminine radar felt certain that he was as curious about me as I was about him.

A Winter Solstice Wedding

I T WAS JUST A FEW MONTHS LATER, when I braced myself and blurted out, "Sir, I want to get married." I was speaking to the Yogi from the phone at the ranch in Espanola. I had been alone in the main house when he called me from Los Angeles. Feeling a need for support because of what I was planning to say, I had stretched the spiral cord attached to the telephone receiver as far it would go, so I could lean against the laundry-room countertop.

I had been primarily living in New Mexico for the past year. The official explanation for why I was stationed there was to establish Espanola as the alternate 'headquarters'. But I couldn't avoid the nagging sense that the Yogi had abandoned me on an emotional level. It was obvious that his other staff members were filling the intimate space I once thought was exclusively mine. I wasn't supposed to think that way, but I did. And it was a very familiar feeling, a deeply sensitive, personal and painful one.

I had plenty of work to fill all of my days and nights, managing events like the Summer and Winter Solstice gatherings, editing Beads of Truth, our community's quarterly magazine, and heading up the Khalsa Council, while the Yogi was traveling with one secretary or another nearly every weekend, teaching White Tantric Yoga all over the U.S. and Europe. But emotional abandonment was what I felt nonetheless.

Within the first few months of meeting the Yogi, he had told me with great certainty, with absolute authority, "Premka, it is not in your destiny to marry. You have only one option and that is to serve me. You have to do my laundry and wash my floors. It is the only way you can clean your karma. I am just looking into the Akashic records[19], and I am just telling you what I see."

The first time he said them, his words had reduced me to tears. They struck me at the core, like they had been delivered by God Himself. I felt the bitter-sweet wrench of sacrifice, knowing I had to willingly give up the possibility, forever, of falling in love with a mortal man, of bearing children, of raising a family.

The sweet part was that it also simplified life a great deal, to have a spiritual teacher who could tell me what God wanted from me. I was already hopelessly in love with Yogi Bhajan, but that was different, and hopeless is the right word. He was guru, God's own channel, and therefore a kind of father-figure. He was also a married man, with three children.

Now, here I was, blurting out this request, in total contradiction to all that the Yogi had told me over the years. On the other end of the line, the Yogi was at first silent, then he finally asked, "Who is there to marry with you? There is no one who is a match for you, I don't think so."

With a slight quaver in my voice, I replied "I have someone in mind, sir."

Silence… then, "Who is that?"

"Siri Brahma." It was quite outrageous of me, since Siri Brahma and I had never even had a personal conversation. But arranged marriages had become a very accepted part of our lifestyle. I was counting on the fact that the Yogi could tell one of his devoted students to do anything, and it would not be questioned. And, I was pretty certain that Siri Brahma would be agreeable anyway. From

---

[19]   In theosophy and anthroposophy the Akashic records are a compendium of all human events, thoughts, words, emotion, and intent ever to have occurred in the past, present or future. They are believed by theosophists to be encoded in a non-physical plane of existence known as the etheric plan. —Wikipedia

the first moment we met, I had sensed the attraction between us.

There was a long pause on the other end of the phone before he asked, "Have you spoken with him about this?"

"No sir, I have never spoken with him. There hasn't been any contact between us. But he's close to my age and he's very devoted to you. I think it would be a good option for me so that I could remain as Secretary General but live separate from your household."

He quietly and calmly replied, "Ah, you know Premka, he doesn't even like women? You didn't know that? I don't think this would work out well for you."

That was an unexpected complication. It had never occurred to me that he might be gay. And if it was true, it was certainly not what I was hoping for. But I was feeling pretty desperate to escape the pain and confusion of living in Yogi Bhajan's household. So I quickly replied, "I don't care. I don't care if he's gay, I don't care if we never have sex. That's not what's important to me. I just want to have a separate life, away from all of the pettiness surrounding you."

He laughed and I could already feel my resolve weakening under his relentless reminder, "No one can accept the Secretary General being married to an ordinary man. This will not work out. You just get yourself ready and join me in Florida for our Winter Solstice gathering. Whole family is coming to Orlando and we have a job to do, both of us. Just get yourself packed up and come and be with me."

Whenever he said 'we', whenever he embraced me in that inclusive statement about 'our mission' and when I felt the possibility of being close to him again, I was hooked. Emotions. Great tides of emotion. On the one hand I longed to be near the Yogi again, just sitting in his presence as he powerfully orchestrated one life after another, spellbound by his words that inevitably reignited my passionate commitment to the mission. The 'mission', where we were an international community, exemplifying how to live a yogic lifestyle with God-centered practices and committed family values, where divorce was not an option, with respect for women, dedication to our children and the generations to follow. It was a lofty vision and I truly believed it was what we offered to a world that desperately needed it.

Then another tide of emotion would roll in and I would long to break free, to have a life that wasn't controlled by the whims of an all-powerful spiritual teacher who didn't follow any of his own rules.

A few days later I was flying to Orlando. I was, after all, the primary organizer for these yearly events that were attended by 300-500 students and student-teachers from around the world. This Winter Solstice gathering was being held in a YMCA campground on a small lake outside of Orlando. The original reason for holding Winter Solstice events in Florida was based on the expectation that it would be warm in December. This inevitably turned out to be a disappointing expectation indeed. Ten days and nights of camping in tents, next to a lake, in Florida in the wintertime—it was bitter cold! Attendees had to wear gloves and long underwear, and even boots were desirable for the hike to the port-a-potties and limited restroom facilities. There was a large kitchen that was adequate to prepare meals for everyone. There were also a few rustic cabins, but they were mostly reserved for the Yogi and his staff members.

All meals were served outdoors. There were no large meeting halls at this YMCA campground. For each meal, everyone lined up in long, straight rows, usually wrapped in a sleeping bag or a wool blanket or two, as servers walked down the lines and distributed large pails of hot food that was intentionally loaded with fresh ginger, garlic and onion. This was the Yogi's recipe to increase circulation, raise body temperatures and protect attendees against potential colds and flus.

"Sat Nam ji?" would be the query before the big ladle would plop out the hot mush-like kitcheree, otherwise known as mung beans and rice. The reply would usually be the same words, but uttered as an affirmation, "Sat Nam ji!" Talking was kept to a minimum, as most of the days of this 10-day event were meant to be observed in silence.

Most of the busy daytime hours were taken up with classes in kundalini yoga, now led by student-teachers, or with White Tantric Yoga that could only be taught by the Mahan Tantric. This was another title that the Yogi had assumed early in his time in the U.S. when he told us, "At any one time on the planet, there is only one Mahan Tantric. This responsibility came to me when my master, Lama Lilan Po, passed away. I got the message in my meditation. There is nothing I can do about it. When it is my time to depart this earth, then I must also pass this title to the student who has prepared himself to carry it on."

Evenings at these Solstice gatherings were my favorite times. Everyone gathered under the stars, facing towards the stage, where an elaborate sound system amplified the exquisite music that had evolved as part of our community. The nights were the time to share old and newly composed songs, with the instruments and musical styles ranging from rock-n-roll guitars to devotional kirtan with harmonium and tabla. Sometimes groups from different regions of the US or from different countries, would perform skits that might poke fun at our lifestyle or some of the more rigid and fanatic idiosyncrasies of our evolving community. Stories would be shared as well, about people and events. We were building a family history.

Huddled together for warmth and lit by the stage-lights, the heart of this family would be visible in the radiant, laughing and joyful faces of students, of devoted followers whose ages spanned up to three generations, with children and sleeping infants cuddled up at the side of parents or grandparents.

Toward the end of the Solstice gatherings there were always group weddings. These weddings were often full of surprise matches.

This particular year was no exception, as one morning I was surprised when the Yogi sent for Siri Brahma to come to his cabin.

As soon as Siri Brahma settled into the room, the Yogi called to one of the women who had been sitting in the circle surrounding him, "Hey you, my 'big brain', Sat Kaur! Come, I want to ask if you know this guy, this Siri Brahma Singh? I know that he is pretty new and he needs more practice to tie a perfect turban. His beard has not even fully grown in, but aside from all that, what you think of him?"

Her face flushing a bright red, Sat Kaur stammered out a response "I don't know, sir. He seems like a good man, sir. But you know that I am very committed to my career, sir. So I don't know what you are thinking, sir?"

Sat Kaur had been around the Yogi for many years, and she had a great sense of humor with a wild hic-upping kind of laugh. She was balancing her resistance to what she suspected was coming, with the addition of 'sir' at the end of each sentence. There were about a dozen people in the Yogi's cabin that morning, part of the circle who had the special privilege of hanging out around him. Everyone got a laugh out of her nervous but humorous response.

The Yogi continued, "Well, I know that you have all kinds of degrees and you are Dean of Women Students at UC Berkeley, and all that blah-blah-blah. And he might not be having this kind of degrees like you, but I am just thinking this is a good match. I'm just thinking that you both should get married."

My stomach clenched with the full realization of what he was doing.

Sat Kaur stayed humorous, "You mean to each other, sir? We don't really know each other, sir. You know that I'm working on my PhD, sir, and you know that I was really planning to **not** get married, sir. And sir, he lives in L.A. and I live in Berkeley. I can't really leave Berkeley, sir."

Yogi Bhajan's response was quick "You want to make God laugh? Tell Him your plans. There is no need to move anywhere for now. You can have a long-distance courtship... after you get married. I am just suggesting that this will be a good match, and I want you to go and talk with each other and just make your decision. We are having a wedding on the final morning. I am requesting the Secretary General to be the minister for this wedding. Go, go, go. Talk, then let me hear that you have come to the right decision."

Although I had officially been a Sikh Minister since the summer of 1972, I had never performed a wedding. Clearly the Yogi was using this opportunity to seal the deal. Having me perform the wedding ceremony was his way of securing my complicity in this marriage that would make Siri Brahma Singh unavailable.

I also knew that I was being tested. The Yogi was testing to see if I was still going to obey him, follow my spiritual teacher's instruction, testing to see if I would carry out my duties, and execute my role in spite of my personal desires. At that time, in 1976, I was not ready to totally oppose him. I was psychologically and spiritually invested in him and in all that had manifested around us. I also had a strong internal judge that took every opportunity to criticize me and fault me for not fully trusting my teacher.

It was perfect irony that Siri Brahma Singh and Sat Kaur came to me shortly after that meeting, seeking my counsel regarding this unexpected turn of events. Sat Kaur had the most hesitation about getting married, while Siri Brahma had a simple way of working with it: "I am a devotee, so whatever my teacher tells me, that's what I'll do. It's simple for me."

This surrendered, calm quality was undoubtedly a big part of my attraction to Siri Brahma. I wished that I had been able to find that simplicity for myself. I had long aspired to such a clear, unwavering commitment. What a relief that would be—to be free from conflict and duality.

The truth was, as the years had passed I doubted my teacher more and more. I sometimes questioned his motivations, I felt conflicted about his tactics, I wondered about the basis for his decisions. I thought I saw pure unadulterated ego at times. We would have our battles, when I would speak with him privately and raise my objections or challenges to things he was doing, decisions he was making. He always won these skirmishes though, and I inevitably came away from any attempt to confront his behavior, regretting that I had once again fallen victim to my doubting mind. These confrontations left me feeling like an utter failure as a devotee. I would silently vow to do better in the future and I was always relieved when he gave me another chance.

In spite of all those doubts and my inner conflict, I encouraged Sat Kaur and Siri Brahma Singh to follow the guidance of their spiritual teacher. That was what was expected of me. That's what was expected of them. It was how things were done in our community, in the culture that had been created over the previous eight years.

The wedding was scheduled for 5am on the tenth and final day of the solstice gathering. The indoor space had been lovingly decorated by other Solstice participants, with green pine boughs and flowers, with sheepskin rugs for each of the couples to sit on. These were arranged on the floor in a semi-circle, with everything oriented toward the Sikh scripture. It was there, surrounding and covering the scriptures, that the decorations were most elaborate. The holy book was covered in layers of silk brocade in brilliant crimson, ornately trimmed with Indian-style golden borders. It sat enshrined within a throne-like frame of shiny brass. The fragrance of burning incense filled the air, along with the mouth-watering smell of freshly made prasad, a traditional sweet pudding made from honey, butter and flour. That prasad was the only thing warm inside the rustic cabin, with its exposed single-wall construction and open rafters.

Numb with cold and stuffed emotions, I sat facing the couple. Alongside me were the three musicians, playing the two harmoniums and one set of tablas[20]. Alternately, the granthi who sat behind the scripture, dramatically folded back the ornate cloth that covered the scripture, and resoundingly recited a round from the Lavan, known as the 'Wedding Song'. Then, the musicians played the musical raga, accompanied by their blended voices, singing the same scriptural verse in the original Gurmukhi language.

Then came my turn, to read out the English translation of each round from *Peace Lagoon*. The entire Lavan utilizes the metaphor of marriage and commitment to one's partner, as the process of committing to 'the Beloved' and thus awakening to the God within. For each round, the couple rises and circles the scripture, the woman following behind the husband-to-be, both walking with heads bowed. Over the course of about 45 minutes, we finally arrived at the closing round:

> *In this fourth round,*
> *The mind grasps the knowledge of the divine,*
> *And God is realized within.*
> *By the Guru's grace we have reached the Lord with ease;*
> *Our bodies and our souls are filled*
> *With the tender delight of the Beloved.*
> *I am a sacrifice unto my Lord.*
> *God seems sweet to me and I have become pleasing*
> *   to my Master.*
> *He fills my thoughts all night and day.*
> *I have obtained the object of my heart's desire—my Lord.*
> *By praising His Name I have gained the highest praise.*
> *The Lord Himself becomes one with His holy bride,*

---

[20] A set of two hand drums

*While the heart of the bride blooms and flowers with
His holy Name.
Slave Nanak proclaims that in the fourth round we have
found the Eternal Lord.*

The ceremony was meditative, soothing, and served to remind me of my own priorities. I longed to break free of my painfully dualistic mind. I wanted to simply love the mystery I had come to call God and to serve the Dharma by living selflessly. My doubts and duality tormented me. I wanted that torment to end. Surrendering to God's Will, sacrificing my personal wants and desires, was the way I was being taught. I accepted that I was the problem, and so I sought to overcome my nagging doubts and questions about my teacher's behaviors. *He was not the problem—I was the problem. Right?*

As the ceremony came to a close, rings were exchanged, partners embraced each other and it was my ministerial duty to finally pronounce Siri Brahma and Sat Kaur, as husband and wife. Now it was done.

That same morning, I was booked on an early return flight to New Mexico. Siri Brahma, as security guard, had previously been scheduled to drive me to the airport and now Sat Kaur, officially his wife, came along as well. As he alone escorted me the final stretch right up to the gate, Siri Brahma spoke softly, "You know, if I had my choice, it would have been you."

Quietly, with my head slightly bowed and not looking at him, I whispered a barely audible, "I know."

Siri Brahma Singh:
Take Two

SORTING THROUGH MY BELONGINGS, separating out laundry to hand over to hotel attendants at the Taj Mahal Hotel, I nervously anticipated the arrival of Siri Brahma. I felt a combination of excitement and anxiety as I heard his knock on the door. I reminded myself that I was simply receiving a treatment from Siri Brahma, security guard and healer. But I was also feeling the current of rebellion that had been ignited in Singapore, and the unique connection that I still felt with this man.

Over the past six years, Siri Brahma had become a friend and a protector to me. After his marriage ceremony that Winter Solstice six years ago, we had never spoken of any personal feelings for one another. For the first few years of his marriage to Sat Kaur, she had remained in Berkeley while he had taken up the leadership of the Pomona Ashram and the Kundalini Research Institute (KRI) that was based there. Her absence had left him free to frequently serve as a security guard for the Yogi, which kept him commuting to Los Angeles and in close proximity to the staff. After a few years of that long-distance courtship, Sat Kaur finally joined him in Pomona. Then more recently, the two of them had moved to Los Angeles together.

As I opened the door of my hotel room to let him in, our greeting was formal and controlled, with eyes averted. I had already changed into comfortable yoga pants and top. I had set out my personal sheepskin rug on the floor and now I explained to Siri Brahma why I had asked him here, "I'm feeling sciatic nerve pain, running down both sides, and it seems to be coming from my low back. I think my hips are out of alignment."

Instructing me to lie face-down on the sheepskin, he placed his hands on my back—his gentle but strong, sensitive hands. I felt my whole being relaxing under his touch, as I was overcome by an oceanic sense of longing. The pain and sadness of my last encounter with the Yogi in Singapore, was very fresh and I was feeling lonely and lost.

It didn't take much, just a few seconds, and the dam that was holding back my emotions gave way. Lying there, face down, the tears began to flow. No words, just grief and sadness and confusion and longing all were rising up and pouring out through my tears.

"Could you please hold me?" I finally asked. Siri Brahma had been kneeling silently on the floor next to me. Not really waiting for him to reply, I sat up and leaned into him. It felt so reassuring to put my head on his shoulder, to rest against his chest, to feel his strong, masculine arms encircling me. I was consumed by a huge sense of loneliness, feeling so cut off from human contact. As I expected, he didn't ask any questions. He simply honored my request. I continued to sob with his arms around me, without words, until the floodwaters gradually subsided.

He held me and I let myself be held. The part of me that had to always keep up a strong image and perform my duty, carry my responsibility, was giving way to the emotional being, the woman, who had all but died under the weight of it all. I was feeling her now, her pain and her isolation.

Over the years, the Yogi often said to me, "Premka, you must be a man. You must just be me. I am going to leave all of this responsibility to you, and you must not be emotional. You know that I have looked at your destiny and it is not written for you to have a personal life. You must just be in service. It is your only option."

I thought about those statements, and it all just felt so totally impossible and even wrong. *How could I be a man? Why must I be a man? If I am destined to be the one to lead this community, then shouldn't I be able to do it as who and what I am? Why would God require a woman to be a man? And the Sikh religion is a householder religion. Everyone is expected to be married, so why wouldn't that be appropriate for me?*

Siri Brahma continued to hold me as these opposing thoughts and feelings swirled inside of me. I felt so safe with him. Such a relief. Still, he was now a married man, and I was committed to my teacher and the mission. I remained in the comfort of his arms until I could stop crying.

Throughout that contact, neither of us dared to speak. I was well trained to never speak to anyone about my feelings, about my private thoughts or my internal struggles. Finally, without even letting our eyes meet, I pulled away from his dutiful and tentative embrace. I once again lay face down and Siri Brahma worked his Jin Shin magic on me. He lightly touched the appropriate combination of meridian points and the energy flow between the points seemed to relieve the pain of my body, while the emotional release of all those tears helped to bring me some momentary sense of peace and calm. Each of us held ourselves with great reserve as I finally thanked him and showed him to the door.

We all remained for a few more days in Delhi, indulging in the luxury of the Taj Mahal Hotel, enjoying room service as well as some of the fine restaurants on the main floor. Once we were sufficiently refreshed, we made our farewell visit to the Golden Temple in Amritsar, re-joining the rest of the group and a few days later we were flying back to the U.S.

Settling back into life in Los Angeles, I immersed myself in practicing and performing Gurbani Kirtan, and continuing my studies of Gurmukhi. Although I was unhappy in my personal relationship with the Yogi and with being part of his household and staff, I was very attached to the Sikh practices and to this community of people who had come to be my family.

Over these past 14 years, I had watched people who were drawn by the kundalini yoga classes that were widely offered. Then I watched as they came to meet Yogi Bhajan and were inspired, with his prodding, to become teachers and finally Sikhs. I had witnessed so many of them as they took their marriage vows, then rejoiced as their children were being born. I watched most of it from a distance, the distance created by my duties and the role I played.

I often watched from behind the lens of my Nikon camera— more of an observer than a participant. I delighted in photographing the innocent faces of newborns or beginning toddlers peering out of neatly turbaned heads, stumbling up to the Guru (the scripture), with their parents faithfully guiding them to make their offerings. Moms or dads would gently push the little turbaned heads to the ground in their first introduction to bowing before God and Guru. From that vantage point, through the eyes of my inner artist and my dedicated idealist, it all looked so adorable, so appealing—a whole new generation growing up with these teachings, with this devotion to God, and with a huge international family as part of their heritage.

I had also witnessed many of the people I had known the longest, heads of ashrams, members of the Khalsa Council, as they came to some crossroad in their lives, where they found themselves compelled to make an independent choice, one that didn't fit with the ever stricter and more confining rules defining the community. I was heartbroken whenever someone finally took off the turban and left, often in the dark of night.

Each departure was quickly condemned by the Yogi. He would explain it away by describing a side of them we hadn't noticed before, a whole new, fatally flawed image of them. Through the power of his words, one of our previously exalted peers would be transformed into a pariah, and effectively cut off from the whole community. With each departure, my own doubts about my teacher, and a torrent of self-questioning would rise up anew. At times I felt I was hanging on to my path, to my place in this lifestyle community, by the sheerest of threads.

Following the incident in Singapore, I sought to get all of my personal needs met through my spiritual practices, through the bitter-sweet joy of self-sacrifice, through my work and through meditation, singing and chanting. I began carving out a life for myself that didn't totally center around the Yogi.

Whenever he was in town, it was routine for members of the Yogi's family and staff to gather in the evening in his sitting room. There he was naturally the center of all activity, either offering insight and commentary about current events in response to the news on television, or lecturing to those present, or complaining about someone, usually about his staff. Food and drink were always being served—a huge part of the Sikh tradition. 'Guest equals God', and food must be served—it was absolutely mandatory.

I had grown increasingly impatient with sitting there, with listening to things I had already heard him say any number of times. Instead I was now choosing to be absent during many of these evenings. I remained in my own room at the Estate, practicing kirtan or studying the Punjabi language. This change in routine did not go unnoticed by the Yogi, and one day he remarked, "Ah, Premka thinks she is more holy than me these days."

Yogi Bhajan had often declared that his job was "to make you ten times greater than me", yet none of us would ever presume to compare ourselves to him. So this remark of his was actually a huge insult and I defensively responded, "Sir, I'm just trying to learn kirtan and Gurmukhi. I love the Guru and the Dharma. I would think you would be happy about that. I'm not trying to be more holy than anyone."

I understood that his remark was intended to point out an error in my ways, to prod me back into line. There was a time when I would have immediately stopped any outside activities to get back into his good graces. But these days I was less and less influenced by his criticism.

Shadows on the Sand

S IRI BRAHMA WAS ALSO RESUMING HIS LIFE in Los Angeles and he was finding new ways to be of service to me. Over the years, as the number of women who made up Yogi Bhajan's staff increased, he had begun requiring that we be escorted or accompanied by a trusted male escort when venturing out of the immediate vicinity. As part of the official security team, Siri Brahma approached me one morning with an offer, "Ji, if you need someone to accompany you to take your morning run, just let me know. I would be happy to do that."

Did I really need a security guard to go for a run in the neighborhood? I had grown accustomed to running by myself. Meanwhile, the Yogi constantly emphasized our safety, and having company on my morning run would be more interesting than going alone, so I replied, "Thank you, that might be good. I guess we could plan on some mornings after sadhana."

"Sure, just let me know. By the way, Sat Kaur and I are going to Santa Monica beach after Gurdwara on Sunday. Would you like to go along with us?"

It was unusual to have someone in the congregation invite me somewhere—quite out of character and routine, because the members of the staff were effectively segregated. That was especially true for me. But I was exploring more and more freedom these days, so I replied, "That sounds wonderful. A walk on the beach would be a nice change. I miss the ocean, I hardly get there anymore." Nature had been my place of solace when I was young, whereas my current position and duties left little opportunity for leisure or recreation.

Since the invitation had included his wife, I felt I was within the boundaries of our staff protocol when I accepted his invitation. As it turned out, Siri Brahma was a long-time surfer and he brought along some Boogie-Boards and gave me my first lessons in bodyboarding. I had a blast.

Following that exhilarating lesson, Siri Brahma, Sat Kaur and I walked together along the beach. It was now late afternoon and the sun was at our backs. In front of us was the image of our shadows on the sand. Whereas I was virtually always covered from head to toe, in turbans and silk chunis, long churidars and kurtas, now, after our swim, we were wearing only our bathing suits. My waist-length hair was hanging loose.

As I looked at our shadows on the sand, I was suddenly struck at the sight of my own feminine form—the curve of my waist and hips, with long flowing hair drifting off to one side. It was a lovely image, a very feminine reflection. As I observed it, I was overcome with sadness because I hardly recognized my own female form as having anything to do with who I had become. I was engulfed by a deep grief, a profound sadness for the woman in me, as the Yogi's words repeated in my head, "Premka, you have to be a man."

Tastes of Freedom

OVER THE YEARS OF 1983-84, whenever I was in L.A., I was able to be more regular about attending the early morning sadhana practices at Guru Ram Das Ashram. It was easier now because I wasn't keeping the Yogi's schedule of eating late and staying up until all hours of the night. Unless there was a pressing invitation from him, I kept to my own schedule. Having the time and energy to rise up in the amrit vela, to sit with other members of the community in the early morning hours, was nourishing to my soul. And in spite of my teacher's biting comments, I refused to feel guilty about this pleasure.

As the winter months approached, the usual time for a trip to India, we received invitations from congregations in southern India, Malaysia and Thailand as well. Each of the congregations was asking for a small group to come and perform kirtan. The Indian Sikh communities were fascinated and inspired at the sight of white Westerners, most of us with blonde hair and blue eyes, playing harmoniums and tablas, singing the Sikh kirtan in their native language. In those huge congregations we were received like pop stars, as thousands of people would show up just to get a glimpse of us. Indian Sikhs would line the streets, pack the temples, even touch our feet, showering us with flowers, food, hospitality and even rupees (the Indian currency).

There were a number of musicians in our international community, many of whom were aspiring ragis (the word for someone who performs music in the Eastern raga style). Some of us had formed a typical team of two vocalists, each playing the harmonium, which was a small keyboard instrument that had a bellows, like an accordion. The third part of this musical jatha (group) was always the tabla player. Tablas consist of two small drums playing a rhythmic contrast to the melody line being played on the harmoniums.

Singing and playing the harmonium had become my personal drug of choice. Now the Yogi called on me saying, "Premka, I think it would be a good idea if you and Ram Das Kaur can prepare to make this journey. You will need to practice more, learn more shabads[21] and get ready to depart very soon."

What good news! Now it seemed that my months of practice and focus were paying off after all. I was very ready for a break from Los Angeles and from the entire scene around the Yogi. And a chance to perform kirtan was the perfect opportunity to do something I loved, removed from all the stress of my other responsibilities.

This particular trip was lining up to be quite unique, for one thing it was going to be three months long, instead of the more typical five-six weeks and we would not only travel to India, but on to Malaysia and Thailand, with a special exploratory trip to Sri Lanka. Plus we would be traveling as a small group of only five of us.

I had been visiting India nearly every year since that first visit in 1970. Each trip was undertaken as an opportunity to bring new yoga students or aspiring Sikhs to experience the Gurdwaras of Punjab, culminating in a visit to the most highly revered Golden Temple of Amritsar. On all of the previous trips, I had a great deal of responsibility for these first-time visitors.

Depending on the political climate of any given year, the Yogi would sometimes come along. However, politics in India were consistently volatile and Yogi Bhajan was always controversial

---

[21] Devotional songs drawn from the Sikh scripture

amongst the Indian Sikhs, ostensibly because he taught both yoga and Sikhism. Most Indian Sikhs regard yoga as an ascetic practice that is contrary to their religion. His break with Maharaj Virsa Singh back in 1971 had also generated ill will in some politically powerful circles. Probably most controversial of all, many Indians believed the Yogi was building a personality cult—a huge contradiction to the Sikh religious tenets.

Uniquely, on this trip I would be traveling with just a handful of secretaries, all of whom had prior experience with India. My kirtan partner was Ram Das Kaur, whose official title was Secretary of Religion. The Yogi created this title for her because she was deeply immersed in the Sikh music and the language of the Sikh scriptures, and even conversational Punjabi. Her passion for the Dharma inspired her to put in many years in study. Her natural inclination and special talent as a teacher made her a valuable resource for the community, as she would teach the rest of us whatever she was learning.

Although she had a title, and was given an office in the Secretariat, she was not considered part of the staff. This distinction was subtle, but important. Staff members (of which we were now 12) were expected to fulfill each other's social needs. But my kirtan partnership with Ram Das Kaur had become more significant to me than those other relationships. I was taking advantage of the fact that she was a dedicated teacher, with great patience and an entertaining sense of humor. It was so wonderful to sing and learn and get high on kirtan with her. In our regularly scheduled practice sessions, we would often crack each other up, usually over some silly mispronunciation, and I would roll on the floor with laughter. I found that laughter was such good medicine and such a relief from the heavy mood that was so prevalent around the Yogi these days.

As the morning for our departure arrived, my phone rang. It was Siri Brahma, asking if he could come and wish me good-bye. That was an unusual request, but I was flattered and felt comforted by his special care and affection for me. I was busy packing and organizing when he arrived. He looked sheepish and shy, as he blurted out another unusual request, "I was wondering if I could give you a good-bye hug?"

In our community, physical contact between men and women was generally discouraged. Our typical way of greeting each other was to offer a slight bow with our hands in a prayer position, Indian style. Hugs were more back-slapping events, between men and men, and any actual body-contact didn't go below the shoulder-level. It was virtually an institutionalized behavior to avoid chest to breast contact, and heaven-forbid that any contact occurs anywhere lower than that! In spite of all that, I let him put his arms around me, as he confessed, "You know, I'm really going to miss you. Please take good care of yourself, you're really important to me."

Oh God, I wish he wouldn't do that! I was accustomed to living in my state of denial, to shutting down to all of my feelings. Now my head was spinning, my heart was pounding. I knew that neither of us was ready to deal with the consequences of how we really felt about each other. There was too much at stake, and nowhere to go with this relationship. We both had commitments that were integral to the fabric of our lives.

I stepped away, stood up straighter, composed myself, and emotionally retreated behind the safety of my role, the safety of the rules. Turning my attention back to the details of packing, I made a desperate attempt to cover the fact that I was drowning in emotions as I assured him, "I promise I'll be fine. This should be a very enjoyable trip, actually. I'm really looking forward to it. Thank you, though, for your concern."

He turned to go, then turned again to ask, "Ji, if you get a chance, I would love it if you would send a postcard or something. That would be really wonderful, to hear from you. You're going to be gone for such a long time."

My world was otherwise so insulated, so sheltered, and so impersonal. Looking back, I can see that was a big part of the attraction to Siri Brahma—he dared to relate to me as a person, as a woman. I was touched by it, as I silently wondered to myself, *"Is he really that courageous or just a fool?"*

Later that night, five of us boarded our flight to New Delhi. Upon our arrival, a customary round of receptions awaited us, along with a schedule of performances. Every trip to India also had its unique features. For this trip it was the journey out of India that was the highlight, with just five of us visiting the tiny island-nation of Sri Lanka, which Indians affectionately referred to as the 'Pearl of the Indian Ocean'. It was still a relatively democratic country then, in 1983. It was predominantly Buddhist, and peaceful.

Everywhere we traveled we saw elephants being used as part of the workforce, serving to move lumber, clear trails, or carry large loads. 'Batik' was the national fabric-art, often featuring ornate images of Tara or Buddha or Hindu images like Krishna or Kali. In the center of the cities, the traffic was directed through round-abouts, like in Europe. But here in Sri Lanka, right in the center of every roundabout was a Buddhist shrine.

I was also very impacted by the experience of entering Sri Lanka. I had many experiences of entering India, where the Customs and Immigration inspectors had strict requirements for incoming visitors to report all electronic equipment and devices, to ensure they would not be sold or gifted to anyone—a means of enforcing their foreign trade policies. India's Customs Inspectors had lots of attitude, very unwelcoming and full of suspicion and they were also widely known to be highly susceptible to bribery!

By contrast, Sri Lanka was very open. There were virtually no constraints, no tensions. We felt warmly welcomed and safe to roam about. On a subtle level, it was another new sensation of freedom.

While in Sri Lanka, we visited some amazing botanical gardens, with gigantic and ancient Banyan trees and all kinds of tropical species of flowers and ferns. My most memorable experience was a spontaneous bare-back ride on some local elephants. Guided by their human caretakers, we rode them into a gently flowing river, my hands in direct contact with the thick, leathery hide that sprouted the occasional thick and stiff, wiry hairs. I loved these gentle giants and was deeply impacted by this personal contact.

I loved Sri Lanka and being there was more like a vacation than anything I had known over my nearly 16 years with Yogi Bhajan. We briefly connected with the few Sikhs who lived there, but most of our time was spent in a totally new experience for me—some freedom of movement. I wasn't responsible for a large group. I could actually go sightseeing, enjoy and relax a little.

Confessions and Declarations

THREE MONTHS LATER, and within hours of my return to Los Angeles, I received a phone call from Siri Brahma. His deep and resonant voice touched me as he said, "Sat Nam, ji, welcome back." I heard his characteristic and slightly self-conscious chuckle, as he went on, "I just thought to offer, since you are still on Indian time, that Sat Kaur and I could escort you if you feel like going to a movie at some strange hour, or if you need a late-night meal."

Feeling reassured by the inclusion of his wife, I appreciated his thoughtful offer. "Wow! That might be a good idea. I actually want to see 'Gandhi'." The film had debuted while we were out of the country.

"Yes, it's supposed to be a really great film. We haven't seen it yet either."

"Well, I'll let you know if I can't get to sleep tonight." In Los Angeles the time was already 8 pm when I called to take him up on the invitation. Siri Brahma and his wife were soon there to escort me.

On another of those first nights back in L.A., Siri Brahma again called, this time to invite me to dinner. It was a spontaneous invitation, and I accepted, suggesting that we meet at my favorite Chinese restaurant on La Cienega Blvd. Pulling up to the front entrance, the valet opened my door, taking my keys and parking my car for me. I spotted Siri Brahma, waiting at the restaurant's front door with his hands folded in front of him. He opened the door for me and we were guided by the maître d' to our small table, set with white table cloth and linen napkins.

Inside, the entire ceiling of this restaurant was lined with rows upon rows of round paper lanterns inscribed with Chinese characters and images of flowers blooming along characteristic brown and black brush-stroke branches. I always found it soothing and aesthetically pleasing to sit under their soft and friendly glow.

Once we had been seated, it became clear that it was just the two of us. I inquired, "When you called to invite me, I assumed that Sat Kaur would be coming. Where is she?"

Siri Brahma flashed his characteristic shy smile, allowing his blue eyes to glance up and meet mine, just for an instant. "She is busy writing her PhD thesis, so she wanted to keep working tonight."

Siri Brahma was wearing a nicely shaped white turban, and the knee-length kurta (an Indian-style shirt) with cummerbund. This had evolved over the years to become the standard dress for Western male Sikhs, along with the white churidars. All of the white was contrasted by a dark blue cloth strap that served as a holster for his symbolic 'kirpan', the small Sikh dagger. The kirpan hung openly below his waist, over his left hip. Seven years had passed since he joined our community and he had fully adapted to the Sikh lifestyle by now, with a reddish-brown beard that was exceptionally thick and full.

I felt safe and protected with Siri Brahma. He treated me with great reverence and respect, with a slightly exaggerated formality, pulling out my chair and eager to attend to me. Trained in martial arts, and instinctively devotional, he had recently taken on the role of 'head of security' for the Yogi. His masculine presence was always reassuring to me.

We shared my favorite spring rolls and snow peas with water chestnuts, over steamy and fluffy white rice. He asked a few questions about our trip and I enjoyed describing the beauty of the island country of Sri Lanka. Then, as we sat enjoying our tea, Siri Brahma cleared his voice self-consciously and blurted out, "You know, Ji, for a long time I have wanted to tell you that I am in love with you ... I have been, ever since I first met you ... I know there is really nothing to be done about it, but I just really wanted to let you know."

I nearly choked on my hot tea! Oh my God, it was totally unheard of for anyone to speak to me in such a personal way. My duty seemed to require that I reprimand him, that I correct his behavior. I should tell him he shouldn't speak to me this way. Perhaps I should be outraged and insulted and get up and walk away?

But he had just done something very gutsy—he had dared to reveal his feelings for me. I certainly couldn't let him know that I felt the same way. All I managed to say was, "Uh yes, it's true that there really isn't anything to be done about that."

I was in shock. I was Premka, I was the Secretary General, I was part of Yogi Bhajan's staff, and nobody, but nobody, ever dared to address me in such a personal way. Now, the fact that he was saying this to me, that he was confessing that he loved me, was opening up floodgates of barely repressed emotions—feelings about how very much I wanted to be loved, to be held, to have a husband and a family.

My own relationship with Yogi Bhajan had changed so much over the years. I had resisted the change from personal attendant to administrator, but my protests were futile. He simply increased his descriptions of the role he saw for me. More and more frequently he stressed to me that the whole future of the Dharma depended on me. I no longer lived in the same house with him, I almost never traveled with him anymore, and I rarely had any moment alone with him.

When I would try to talk to him about my unhappiness with my isolation, or with having no time with him, he was quick to silence me by repeating and reinforcing a theme, "Premka, you must understand that I have put you on a pedestal. Haven't I always warned you that it is lonely at the top? You think I don't understand?

Do you know how painful I am that I have no peers? But I'm just preparing this huge 3HO family for you. I'm just doing all of this for you, you must understand. I have given you so much position and respect. One day, after I am gone, the whole mission will be resting on your shoulders. I think you should meditate more, and just pray that Guru should bless you to be in gratitude."

It was true. I didn't feel much gratitude. And after such lectures, I also felt guilty for being so imperfect, for behaving like another emotional female, making personal demands on him. However, these days I was feeling more and more that the pedestal he described for me was really more of a prison cell.

As I continued to try and compose myself after his surprising confession, Siri Brahma took care of our check. I had been careful not to reveal any of my own emotions in response. Now, I felt an urgent need to get back to the safety of my room, to the solitude of Guru Ram Das Estate. *What is the right way to handle this?* I had a tidal wave moving through me. His declaration had unleashed emotions I didn't know I was capable of feeling: possibilities, hope, love, longing. *Oh my God, he felt the same way about me as I felt about him.* I had to find a way to handle this—on my own. I obviously couldn't go to the Yogi for a solution, and I had absolutely nowhere else to turn.

One thing you could say about our family, about our community, we were very adept at denial and repression. Of course, we didn't really have such words or concepts back then. Instead we were taught to cover over things with spiritual words like 'duty' and behaving 'gracefully'. Ironically, we said 'Sat Nam' while we covered our true thoughts or feelings. 'Sat Nam' is the greeting the Yogi had taught us. 'Sat' means truth. 'Nam' means name or identity. The translation: "Truth is my name—it is my identity. Truth, the Ultimate Truth is who I truly am."

As a teenager I had resented my parents' way of coping with

emotions and unpleasant situations, by ignoring them, by not talking about them. I had given it a name back then—I called it 'ostrich behavior'. I was beginning to see that this new family that I had found, this replacement for the one that I had violently rejected as a teenager, had the same behaviors: *Don't talk about the gnarly stuff—don't deal with your emotions, just sweep issues and conflicts and doubts and mistakes, under the carpet. Keep it all neatly wrapped in white cloth, hide it under layers of cotton turbans and silky chunis.*

It was not just that the individuals in this 3HO family behaved this way, this behavior was virtually institutionalized. Much of what was passed down to us as the teachings of Yogi Bhajan was culturally adopted right out of Indian society. And Indian society had been greatly influenced by British society. We had even developed a written set of Codes of Conduct, and we had teachings for everything, from child-raising to brushing our teeth and sitting on the toilet.

As I quickly drove myself back to Preuss Rd., I was pursued by Siri Brahma Singh's declaration. I could feel my own dutiful resolve caving in, as a huge question rose up from some core place inside me, and smacked me upside-the-head: *"Why would everyone else's happiness depend on my being deprived and **unhappy?** Why was I supposed to carry on this huge responsibility without being allowed to have a husband, a partner? How does it make sense that I was being required to be the head of this householder religious community while not being allowed to be married?"*

With all of these doubts and questions swirling, along with the huge groundswell of emotion unleashed by Siri Brahma's words, I arrived back at Guru Ram Das Estate. Hurrying to get to the privacy of my room, once there I fell to my knees, forehead on the floor in front of my altar, praying for help, for guidance and renewed faith. Desire was pulsating through me. I wanted him, I wanted to run into his arms and feel held, feel loved. My imagination of what it would be like to give in to our long-suppressed desire for one another was consuming—so powerful that I also sensed it was inevitable—and that was terrifying. I was not willing to lose this family by falling from grace like so many before me. I was caught in a dilemma that seemed to have no way to resolve itself.

There was only one conclusion really, regardless of my own desires, regardless of the fact that I knew Siri Brahma had been pushed into his marriage in order to keep him away from me. Now, the fact was that I must be more careful to keep Siri Brahma at a distance. Truly, there was nothing that could be done about our feelings for one another. I must simply keep my attention focused on my own meditations, my studies of the language and the scripture, and my kirtan practice.

My relationship with Ram Das Kaur was filling some of the emotional gap, since I was more and more estranged from the rest of the staff. I was making that choice because I was no longer willing to play the game of seeking the Yogi's attention and approval. As much as possible, I stayed away.

On the infrequent occasions when I did show up in the evening, I found him to be increasingly agitated. He looked bitter, always complaining. It was painful to be around, seeing his face and even the color of his complexion darkened by scowls and constant frowning. It was also hard not to take his remarks personally, as he would lash out, seemingly indiscriminately declaring, "I have a staff that is too emotional. You all lay your trips on me—instead I should be able to lean on you. That is what a staff is for, to give me support. You are supposed to serve me, help me to carry out my Guru's mission. Instead you treat me like an ordinary man, like a boyfriend." He would then dramatically crank down the foot support on his recliner chair and march off to the bathroom, throwing out a last exasperated remark: "I think I must make some changes. Anyone who wants to leave me, just pack up your belongings and get going. I'll be fine. My Guru will provide. After all, it is His mission."

Whatever specific event might have triggered these tirades, the Yogi would rarely name anyone. His vagueness left each of us to wonder if we were the one to blame, each shrinking in self-examination and self-criticism. Or, maybe someone knew they were the trigger for tonight's outburst and would be inwardly praying to not be named in front of the others. Often there were male witnesses to all of this drama, like Hari Jiwan, his Chief of Protocol, or Dr. Saram or Dr. Alan Weiss, two of the medical doctors who were kept close to the inner circle. More than witnessing, they seemed to form a kind of men's club, all of them understanding the frustration of dealing with 'women'.

I was relieved by my decision to stay away, in spite of the distance it was creating between me and the rest of the staff. Now my evenings were filled with kirtan practice, often with Ram Das Kaur, while my mornings sometimes included a run with Siri Brahma. Although we maintained our proper decorum, the energy running between us was getting palpable, as some of my walls of resistance were crumbling.

One morning during a walk together, in the early spring of 1984, I spontaneously asked Siri Brahma, "So how is your marriage with Sat Kaur?"

He quickly and easily responded, "Oh, it's fine. We're good friends. That's about all it is. We have a good relationship, more like brother and sister."

That morning we were walking through the deep and warm sand of Santa Monica Beach. It was a beautiful Southern California morning, sunny and warm, with clear blue skies, the kind of spring day that makes you sense life renewing itself, full of the hope of new possibilities. My spontaneous question was the most personal exchange we'd had since the night in the Chinese restaurant, when he declared he loved me.

Suddenly, like a force of nature, we were in each other's arms, embracing. As words and emotions tumbled out, I exclaimed, "I have this strange sense that I want to have a child with you!" Though I was the one speaking, I was surprised at the audacity of such a statement. Prior to this moment we had never embraced each other, never kissed—so where did that come from?

His response was immediate, "Me too! I keep thinking I want to have a baby with you. It's so strange, because I never even considered having a child in all the seven years I've been married to Sat Kaur."

The dam had burst. Embedded in his statement were many messages, 'I love you, I want to be with you. We belong together.' That's what I heard, that's what I believed. My biological clock was certainly ticking loudly. I was now 40 years old. All I knew was that this urge, this message, was stronger than anything I'd ever felt with any other man. This sense of the child who was asking to be born to Siri Brahma and me, was amazingly palpable.

Now, my passion was combined with my anger, my rage at Yogi Bhajan, because I knew he had deliberately done this to both of us, to all of us. As I felt this swirl of conflicted emotions, I also became even more clear about my determination to move away from the household of my teacher. I imagined that I could move to another city, another ashram. I didn't know if Siri Brahma and I could ever be together, but I was getting clear that I wanted to be free of the control and constraints of living in the Yogi's household. I also really, really wanted to be married, to have a family of my own, to have a life of my own.

I was determined to be free from direct involvement with the Yogi, and from the weight of my empty titles. The hypocrisy and futility of my office was wearing on me and there were many things that had been raising red flags.

Responsibility
Without Authority

FOR SEVERAL YEARS I had been responsible for organizing the council of Sikh Ministers that Yogi Bhajan entitled the Khalsa Council. It was comprised of the specific heads of ashrams that were appointed by him, sometimes including their wives as well. The Yogi directed us to meet four times a year, to set policies and protocols for ministers and plan directions for the international community, the network of ashrams and businesses.

One year, a funding idea was conceived by the Council, to institute a 10% tithing program for supporting the increasing expenses of running Sikh Dharma International. Of course, such donations would be voluntary, but there was a historical precedence for such tithing (known as dasvandh) within the 500-years of Sikh history. As a collection mechanism it was determined that we would rely on every minister or head of ashram to inspire and institute this concept within his local or regional territory. All such tithes would be gathered locally then passed on to the regional directors and forwarded on to International Headquarters.

The Khalsa Council and its procedures had evolved over many years and it was a requirement that the proposals that came out of the Council had to be submitted to the Yogi in his role as Siri Singh Sahib, for his final approval. When the tithing proposal was put before him, he expressed his initial doubts that it would bring in meaningful funding. Nonetheless, he gave his approval for us to go ahead with the idea.

As it turned out, the program became very successful, bringing in thousands of dollars each month. This provided much needed funding to support the ever-growing office facilities and staff members who all lived in the households and worked on the properties of Yogi Bhajan. Up to this point, all income was derived from the Yogi's teaching and travels as well as the yearly family gatherings at the Summer and the Winter Solstices.

As Secretary General for the Khalsa Council, I then assumed it was appropriate for me to prepare financial reports to bring back to the Khalsa Council. It seemed only logical that since the tithing concept had been conceived by the Khalsa Council, they should remain informed. I believed it would inspire these heads of ashrams around the world, to have confirmation that the funding program that we had created was turning out to be so successful. I felt it would demonstrate our self-sufficiency, encourage leadership.

When the Yogi learned from a staff member in the accounting department that I had requested them to prepare such a report, he called me into his presence, declaring, "Premka, I do not want our books to be opened to the Khalsa Council."

I was honestly taken by surprise. The Yogi had told me so often that I was to take leadership and responsibility for the International Headquarters and for the Khalsa Council, so I felt confident I was only doing my job. I argued, "But sir, these are donations to a non-profit, religious organization. We are actually even legally required to show the financial records to the congregation. I feel it is important to show the Council how successful this program has become. There is certainly nothing to hide."

He was equally adamant saying, "Premka, these funds are not the domain of anyone. I am not answerable to these people. I am only answerable to my God. I don't agree that we should show them our accounts. I don't want these people to get into a habit to question me."

I noticed the terminology of 'these people' and was surprised because it was so dismissive. Subtly, 'these people' were being portrayed as other.

"But sir, it's not a matter of questioning you. You have always asked that we take the responsibility and leadership over the entire organization. This successful funding activity is a way to support the International Headquarters. How can we take leadership if we can't even be allowed to look at the finances?"

We fought over this issue for months, but his was always the final word. I never was allowed to report to the Council on the tithing fund.

Several things became apparent to me through that battle. I saw that, with all my titles and constant lectures about my huge responsibility, which I took very much to heart, there was a major contradiction. I actually had no authority. What I had was responsibility, without authority.

Not only did I not have any authority, but I was being told to run an international headquarters office, utilizing a staff that had no real sense of responsibility or allegiance to me.

Whenever my teacher chose to lecture me about my responsibility, he would always refer to the staff as **my** staff. But they were very clearly not. Every member of this staff was hand-picked by him, and each had their lives centered on him. Just below the appearance of a united front, each of us was indirectly pitted against one another, vying for his attention, his affection or his approval.

I also saw that the Khalsa Council was in a similar position to my own. Every member of the Council (about 60 members) was required to attend meetings three or four times per year. Each member had to spend his or her own money for travel and transportation on top of taking time away from their own businesses, although housing accommodations were usually worked out through ashrams and personal connections within the community. Yogi Bhajan made dramatic public statements about the importance and honor of serving on the Khalsa Council, but I was beginning to get a clearer understanding that this revered Council actually had no authority to enact anything.

Again, responsibility with no authority. We could only make a recommendation to Yogi Bhajan. We might spend days or weeks or months hammering out some plan we felt was important to serve the international community, the children, or the future. As it turned out, the Yogi could wipe out all of our hard work with the stroke of his pen. Or he could take the credit, or the benefit, for himself.

Seeing this made all of my dedicated service seem meaningless. I felt isolated from every other person in the community by the very definition of my role, bound up with feelings that I couldn't express to anyone, over-burdened with responsibilities, and my faith in my teacher was indeed being tested.

Still, I was determined that I would not lose this family or my spiritual practice. I had watched so many others be pushed out, I was determined it was not going to happen to me. There was so much that I couldn't share with Siri Brahma: about my personal relationship with the Yogi, about my own personal doubts and the apparent hypocrisy that I witnessed.

Following that first embrace on the beach in Santa Monica, the next weeks were filled with clandestine meetings and secret phone calls. We experienced our first kiss. I was feeling so much of my anger toward the Yogi, that it made me feel bold and rebellious, providing additional fuel for the passion between Siri Brahma and me.

After one of our morning jogs, in that spring of 1984, Siri Brahma walked me back home and I invited him to come inside.

On that particular morning, I knew that we would have the house to ourselves, at least for a short while. Out of an abundance of caution, we sat in the formal dining room, seated side-by-side on a pair of mahogany chairs, each facing towards the front window. This gave us a clear view of the only walkway leading up to the front door of the house, so we would have sufficient warning if anyone approached. I leaned my head onto his shoulder, appreciating the touch of his hand on mine.

There was so much that Siri Brahma didn't know, so much I couldn't really tell him about the issues troubling me. Over the course of the past few weeks we were jogging together in the mornings, flirting, confessing our love and whenever we felt safe enough, we would even hold each other in a passionate embrace. But we had not been sexually intimate and he knew nothing about my own personal relationship with our teacher.

As we allowed our relationship to blossom, I was more certain than ever that I had to make a move. Something had to change and on this morning I decided to share some of my thoughts with Siri Brahma, "Listen, I've concluded that I need to go ahead and resign as Secretary General. I'm going to arrange to talk to Yogi Bhajan and I'm going to request to move away, to the San Diego ashram maybe, or possibly to Eugene, Oregon."

For him, my proposal must have seemed to come out of left field, as he quickly responded, "Why would you do that? You can keep working as the Secretary General. You should ask Yogiji to arrange a divorce for me and Sat Kaur, so you and I can get married. You can still be the Secretary General."

His reply was equally surprising to me. We hadn't ever talked about a future for the two of us. I could imagine that my moving out of L.A. would give space and time for Siri Brahma to make his own independent decisions, about his marriage, about us. Although we were flirting and pushing the envelope, I didn't want to be the reason or the excuse for him to get a divorce.

I tried to explain, "There are lots of things I can't really tell you right now, and many reasons why I don't want to continue as Secretary General. Reasons that have nothing to do with you and me. But apart from that, I didn't know you wanted to marry me?"

He didn't hesitate, "Like I told you after my wedding, if it had been up to me, I would have married you back then."

Not just a little incredulous, I questioned, "So you really think Yogiji could just tell Sat Kaur to get divorced, and that would be okay with her?"

With that same confidence, he said, "Yes, Sat Kaur will agree to anything he asks her to do, and our relationship is more like brother and sister anyway. I've told you that."

It sounded so simple, but I had my own reservations. "Well, there's no way I'm going to ask him. You don't understand what would happen if I did that. He would come after you so fast. You'd be pushed out of this family in a heartbeat. You never knew this, but I already asked him to let me marry you, just before he arranged your marriage to Sat Kaur."

He looked surprised, "No, I didn't know that. So, you felt it too, the energy between us, way back then?"

"Yes, of course I did. But I could never let you know because the Yogi requires his staff members to avoid contact or involvement with any other men."

We carried on this line of discussion over the course of a few days, with him continuing to encourage me to talk to the Yogi even as I repeated my warnings, "If I go speak to him, and if I can't get him to agree, then I know how he operates. We won't be allowed to speak to each other again. You could be sent away, banished from the community, and I'll be watched like a hawk. We'll be cut off from each other. We'd be taking a huge risk."

Then one morning Siri Brahma came to me with a plan that he believed would overcome one of the concerns I had raised, "I'll open a P.O. box at the post office up on Pico Blvd., near the fitness center. We'll both have keys to it, and whatever happens, we can leave each other messages. That way, if things don't go well, we can stay in communication while we figure out our next steps."

This willingness (or was it really ignorance?) on the part of Siri Brahma to step across lines of protocol and reach out to me, made him kind of irresistible. His confident and urgent proposal was offering me something I desperately needed—a partnership and support in making a move. Having a co-conspirator was energizing me to take some concrete steps forward.

Over recent years, in the process of all of my self-questioning and internal evaluation, I had faced some hard and deep questions and hit some core truths. My own urgency about getting away from Yogi Bhajan had everything to do with being true, being in integrity. In reality, I had been compromised for 16 years now—participating with my teacher in a level of deception. I had the excuse that I had given him the authority over my life, my actions. Therefore, I did not perceive myself as culpable. At this point I believed (and feared) that 'truth would ultimately prevail' and the deception would be exposed. Yogi Bhajan's reputation was what was at risk, but mine would surely be destroyed as well.

In stepping up and moving away from the inner circle, I had to be willing to relinquish my status, my titles and my future financial security. But I was finding myself without any real choice. I simply had to be true to myself. I had to feel good about my priorities. That excruciatingly painful decision, to take the risk of losing absolutely everything that had defined me was my most core choice, versus selling out my conscience.

Yogi Bhajan once posed a spiritual challenge to me: "Premka, your trust and devotion must be so perfect, that if I ask you to kill a man, you will just do it, without any hesitation." Though I couldn't believe he was truly serious about this, or that he would ever really ask it of me, I was nonetheless struck by the issue it posed—of total trust. As I gave contemplative, quiet consideration to what he was asking, what I found was revealing.

Sikh history, as with many religious traditions, (notably Judaism and Christianity) is filled with stories of tests of faith. One Guru of the Sikhs was burned alive, seated on hot metal over a burning fire, while hot sand was poured over his head, as he continued to recite the Name of God as defined by the Sikh faith. Another was buried alive. These tortures were carried out by warring Muslims in 16th century India, in an attempt to persuade these Sikh gurus, whom they considered as apostates, to renounce their own beliefs and embrace Islam.

In another famous tale, the last of the ten Sikh Gurus put out a challenge to his followers, asking for the heads of any who considered themselves to be his devoted Sikhs. Only five out of tens of thousands of the disciples who were present that day, had the faith and courage to step forward. Those five became mythic heroes of the Sikh faith as they bowed their heads under his sword. (The miracle of this event was that the five followers did not actually die. They instead re-appeared dressed in the garb of the pure Sikh (Khalsa), and thus became physical and mythological symbols within the Sikh faith.)

These exemplary stories of devotion, faith and sacrifice are core images of the Sikh tradition. Looked at in this context, this challenge by the Yogi might not seem so extreme. Yet his request revealed what was true for me. I thought I wanted this level of faith and devotion, but I realized I did not have it. Not with this teacher.

Filled with such thoughts, stories and images, my meditations over the course of the next few days were not peaceful. I weighed my options, attempting to determine the right course for me to take. Finally, by the end of the week, I called Yogi Bhajan to request a time to speak with him privately. Being highly intuitive and hyper-vigilant to the emotional currents of his all-female staff, he could sense the determination in my voice and the intensity of my request. He didn't try to brush me off.

*And the day came when the risk to
remain tight in a bud was more
painful than the risk it
took to blossom.*

~ ANAIS NIN

Negotiating with a Master

A RRIVING AT GURU RAM DAS ASHRAM for our scheduled appointment, according to the established protocol of the day, the volunteer security guard on duty rang inside via telephone intercom, to announce my arrival. I then used one of my numerous keys to open the dead bolt on the side gate into Yogi Bhajan's private compound. Over the years, the layers of security and gates and bars were ever increasing. So was the size and weight of my key chain.

I listened for the clang of the heavy metal gate as it closed behind me. Deep in thought and feeling the weight of my decision, I passed through the narrow walkway leading to the small living room where the Yogi was seated in his recliner chair. Nirinjan, his personal secretary, was holding out some correspondence for his signature. The television was on, as usual, playing one of his favorite John Wayne westerns.

He briefly looked up, peering over his reading glasses, acknowledging my presence with a nod of his head. I respectfully put my palms together, briefly touched his outstretched feet by way of greeting, and sat down on the couch to wait. Finally, as he lowered the footrest to his recliner and switched off the TV, he signaled with a sideways movement of his head, for me to follow him, "Come along, Premka. Let us talk. Pink Krishna has set my room. We can have privacy there."

Leading the way, he walked back through the kitchen, and out the side door. His graying and thinning hair was tied up in a rishi-knot on top of his head, and he wore no turban. His white sleeveless t-shirt revealed once athletic shoulders that remained nicely rounded in spite of so many years of neglect. Below the line of his t-shirt, some belly protruded over the tie of his big, loose, pure white katcheras[22]. These traditional baggy undershorts reached all the way to his knees. He was otherwise wrapped in his favorite brown woolen shawl, with one end draped over his left shoulder.

I followed a few steps behind him as we walked along the narrow walkway through the little garden courtyard with his custom-designed Jacuzzi pool set amidst his beloved rose garden. We were walking to his private sleeping quarters and meditation space, which was actually a converted garage located at the rear of the property. Leaving our shoes on the small cement porch, we stepped inside, taking turns to bow down before the altar that took up about ten feet of the far wall. In front of the altar were layers of Persian carpets, then sheepskin rugs and his old leopard skin that had accompanied him on his initial journey from India, back in 1968. A tape recorder was playing Gurbani Kirtan, to maintain the vibration.

Securing the door behind us, he pointed for me to sit at one end of his newly re-upholstered white couch. Leaning back at the other end of the couch, he crossed one ankle over his opposite knee, stroked his mustache back from his lips, revealing his small, straight white teeth, and asked, "So Premka, what is happening? Seems to be pretty serious." Everything Yogi Bhajan did had an aura of drama to it. Actually, his whole being was dramatic. Today was no exception.

However, I was beyond being intimidated by any of it. I was feeling resolute, strong in my intention, as I replied, "Yes, that's true. I'm feeling quite serious. This is the second time that I'm asking for this. I want to marry Siri Brahma Singh. He's requesting that you

---

[22] The special under garment that is part of the ritual wear for all initiated Sikhs.

arrange for his divorce with Sat Kaur." I saw the Yogi's face darken with displeasure and, more surprisingly to me, I thought I saw fear.

Still, I went on, "He feels confident you can talk her into agreeing to this. And we both know that you can easily get members of the community to accept whatever story you wish to tell them."

I had fully exposed my position now, and I knew there was no turning back. Whatever the outcome of this meeting, I had broken free of a huge constraint. I went on, "So, if you want to arrange this for us, then things can go smoothly. The way I see it, I could go to the Eugene ashram or to San Diego while their divorce is being finalized. We realize it takes six months for a divorce in California. Once the dust is settled, you can tell everyone that you have decided to marry me to Siri Brahma.

"If you want to arrange things, then I could keep working for the Secretariat. If you're not willing to arrange it, then I'm going to leave the staff anyway. In that case, I can't say what Siri Brahma will do, but I imagine he'll decide to leave Sat Kaur and will eventually follow me."

Before I could finish my last sentence, I was shocked to see my spiritual teacher was down on the floor, about five feet away, on his knees in front of me, with his hands folded, "Please Premka, I beg you not to do this. Everything we have worked for, it will all be ruined. This will never work out with this man. I tell you he does not have the capacity to support you properly. You don't understand that you are accustomed to fine cars and houses and you travel the world in style."

Looking at my teacher while he was down on the floor in front of me, his over-sized belly protruding, his hands folded in a pleading posture, was very disorienting. It made me painfully uncomfortable. But I quickly interrupted what he was saying, "I don't care about any of those material things, and I'm sure we can manage to live just fine."

It was mind-bending, surreal, to see the Yogi down on his knees. I felt humiliation. I had virtually worshiped this man for 16 years, and although I had my issues with him, I had always seen him as larger-than-life, as regal and proud. This was a totally unnatural posture. I wanted him to stop, to sit back on the couch next to me, to have an honest exchange for once. I knew how persuasive he could be. I expected he would try some new tactic, but I wasn't at all prepared for this one!

He remained there, on his knees, as he took another line of reasoning, "Premka, all my years of work, I have built everything around you. Understand, this will be a huge scandal. Nobody could ever accept the Secretary General married to an ordinary man, and especially a married man. I beg you, please not to do this. You must give up this idea, and just re-dedicate yourself to the mission. Understand that entire family is relying on you. Whole mission depends on you."

I recognized that he was playing on my sense of responsibility, repeating his familiar words about my importance. He knew me very well. I was totally attached to this community that had evolved around us. And I was more invested in the image, the myth of my importance, than I knew. Plus, I was thrown off balance by his demeanor, with seeing him like this, so uncharacteristically emotional.

I heard him as he reiterated, "You must give up this Siri Brahma, once and for all. This will bring nothing but disgrace for you, for everyone. I cannot protect you from that. It will bring down the office of the Secretary General."

In spite of the resolve I had come with, I couldn't help considering his words, as I re-stated my request, "It doesn't have to be that way. You can speak with Sat Kaur yourself, and you can persuade her to go ahead and get divorced. She never wanted to get married in the first place. This was all your doing, so I'm sure you can un-do it."

I knew that I needed to convince the Yogi to create the circumstance, the story. I was certain that if he wanted to use his powers of persuasion, he could literally weave the scenario for all of his willing followers. No one ever challenged his version of reality. In fact, he defined their reality.

He again proceeded to make his arguments: "What do you know about this man, this Siri Brahma? You need to understand his psychology, his character. You know he had one affair already, when he was living in Pomona? And now he has just changed careers and is doing bodywork. You think he can be trusted to massage other women and remain faithful to you?"

Listening to this challenge of Siri Brahma's character, I basically dismissed it. After all, the Yogi himself was a married man. More than that, he was virtually the head of a religion and preaching monogamy! I knew about Siri Brahma's affair, and it was certainly a red flag, but I rationalized that it happened years ago, when his new and long-distance wife, Sat Kaur, was still living in Berkeley. Clearly their arranged marriage was not based on romance or passion.

As our exchange continued, it became increasingly clear that the Yogi wasn't going to agree to our request. He was not going to arrange things for us.

I came to this meeting to propose a compromise, a way to remain as the Secretary General, while allowing me to have physical distance from the Yogi, and a personal life for myself. That's what I wanted. I was definitely infatuated with Siri Brahma. I believed I was in love. But his marriage proposal was almost secondary to my urgent desire to get away from all the deception and dysfunction around the Yogi. It offered me a much-needed partnership, and a route to my escape.

I was trying to achieve something that had not previously been done—to break away from the Yogi's inner circle while maintaining my position and my connection to the community and the Sikh faith. I believed I had some bargaining power, based on the Yogi's repeated claim of my importance, of my indispensable role in the evolution of this spiritual community. I had bought into the myth so often repeated by the Yogi.

I looked at him now, still uncomfortable with his pleading posture, wishing he would get up off the floor. As I listened to his arguments, I began to reconsider whether there was anything that would make it tolerable for me to stick it out, to remain in his household, functioning as the Secretary General?

I knew I could only make it tolerable for me to stay if I could get the Yogi to change his ways. If I could use my indispensability as a bargaining chip, perhaps he would agree to modify some of the behaviors that were most unacceptable to me. Over the years the image of the Yogi and of the entire organization had become inextricably linked to mine. I traveled the world as a representative of the Yogi and of the organization. I was recognized as the translator of the scriptures and had even been written up in *Who's Who in Religion*.

Since he clearly was not going to budge, I now felt compelled to go for a different outcome: "Alright, I'm willing to consider giving up my relationship with Siri Brahma. I'll give up this man I love and who loves me, this one possibility of a personal life for myself, and I'll continue to handle the administration. But only if you agree to certain conditions."

As I spoke, my thoughts were forming. I automatically sat up straighter, my head held higher. My assertiveness was surprising even to me as my personal priorities were organizing into crystal clarity: "The way things are now, I can't even do my job. In fact, it's a joke. I'm held responsible and blamed for things that I don't control, for choices and decisions that you make."

I saw a look of relief as he heard that he might have convinced me to let go of Siri Brahma, but I also noted a flicker of surprise pass over him as he heard me talk of putting forth conditions. Quickly regaining his composure, he encouraged me, "Go ahead then, tell me what are your conditions?"

"First of all, you have to agree to leave Siri Brahma alone! You're not to touch him, and you won't tell his wife, Sat Kaur, anything about our relationship! There's no need to tell her, because nothing actually happened between us and it will be over. You will not push him out of the family. You'll leave him alone. Period. Do you understand? Do you agree?" Surprised at my own strength and conviction, I wasn't holding back.

"Okay, I understand. What next?" He had finally come up off the floor onto the couch, which was a relief! I noticed he was leaning forward like he was preparing to spring into action, and I could see by his eye movements and the changed demeanor and body-language, that he was calculating, concentrating on what I was saying.

Because I had already made the decision to let go of my ownership, my place within this multi-million-dollar empire, I felt a powerful sense of freedom. After all, I had nothing more to lose. My next condition was one that was directly in response to the Yogi's behavior over one of his former staff members, Hari Har Kaur. She had recently moved away, left her position on the staff. It had been months since she had moved back to the East Coast, and the Yogi continued to pursue her, trying to convince her to come back. Although he was always tenacious (i.e., obsessive) in pursuing the outcomes he wanted, when it came to Hari Har, this self-proclaimed head of a religion, was acting like a lovesick puppy.

I spelled it out: "You need to stop making such a fool of yourself over Hari Har. You need to stop obsessing over her. She has stated publicly that she wants nothing to do with being a Sikh, or with wearing a turban, or any of the things that define you and this community. Your continuing pursuit of her, your relentless phone calls with her, your chasing after her, is really, really embarrassing. It's humiliating to all your staff. Everyone sees it, how foolishly you are behaving, and it needs to stop." In addition to all the pain it brought me as a woman, I was also ashamed to see him acting so human.

Now, seated on his white couch, the Gurbani Kirtan softly playing in the background, I watched him carefully. Surprisingly, he seemed to be taking me seriously, as he said, "Okay, I understand. What else?"

This next condition got to the heart of the matter for me: "I cannot continue to work with a staff that you call **my** staff, when each one of them has a personal, physical relationship with you. It's totally disruptive to the business of the Secretariat to mix these emotional relationships with the work environment. Everyone is more concerned about who is with you at any given moment, than in fulfilling their jobs. There's no respect for me, because they're all competing and jealous, of me and of each other. And clearly, their loyalty is not to me, it's only to you."

He continued to listen as his eyes kept scanning. He was clearly thinking… or scheming? But I kept going, "I'm telling you to separate out your personal relationships from my staff. You'll have to decide how to do that, who is personal and who is administrative. But I can't continue to carry this responsibility you thrust on me when I have no loyal staff to work with. You need to clean it up. You need to let me have a real staff to work with if you want me to do my job."

He had been listening intently, never interrupting me, which was amazing in and of itself. "Yes, I understand what you're asking. I'll take care of it."

Really? Was he actually going to listen to me? I was surprised at my own strength, at the clarity of these conditions, at how they had spontaneously and clearly formulated, right on the spot. Of course I had been contemplating the dysfunction for a long time, through the months and years of my silent suffering.

I asked him again, "Do you really understand? Do you honestly agree to all these conditions? That's the only way I'm willing to continue as Secretary General or Administrative Director, or whatever you want to call me."

With an air of urgency, he replied, "Yes, yes, I agree to your conditions. Is that it? Are those all your conditions? Is that everything?"

"Yes, that's it. This is what needs to happen. Otherwise, I'll be gone."

He began to appear more agitated. His expression took on a decisiveness. I could tell that he was busy strategizing. He stood up from the couch, then reached his hand out to guide me to a standing position saying, "Okay, Premka, it will all be okay. Now you just go take care of yourself. Go on back home and get some rest. I'll give the news to Siri Brahma. You must agree that you will not ever see him again, from this day forward."

There it was! Just as I had expected! "No, I don't agree to that. I'll speak with Siri Brahma myself. I'm not letting you be the one who tells him. I'll let him know that our relationship can't go any further, but I'm going to speak with him myself, in person."

By now we were both moving toward the door, as he put his hand on my shoulder, instructing me, "No Premka, you must not speak to him. You must just let me handle this."

But I wasn't backing down, "No, I don't agree. Siri Brahma and I need to have closure, and I'm going to speak to him myself."

By now, we had stepped out into the enclosed garden and the

Yogi was striding up the walkway heading back to his sitting room, like a man with a purpose. I was absorbed in feeling a painful mixture of success and failure, in a state of mild disbelief that I had actually succeeded in negotiating these terms. But I had agreed to pay a heavy price; giving up my dream of a normal householder's life with Siri Brahma. I did so because I also knew that Siri Brahma needed to make his own choices and decisions about his marriage, apart from his feelings for me. I did not want to be the reason he left his wife.

I let myself out the heavy side gate, noting the familiar sound of the thick metal as it clanged shut. Engrossed in thought, I slipped into my silver Mercedes, under the watchful eyes of the ever-present security guard seated near the entry door of the ashram.

Pulling away from the curb, I drove the few miles to our recently established P.O. Box, where I left Siri Brahma a brief note:

My dear Siri Brahma Singh. As I feared, I was unable to convince the Yogi to arrange things, and now we won't be allowed to see each other. I pray you will hold on to the Guru. Please don't leave the Dharma. I love you. Premka.

I drove slowly and tearfully back home. Letting myself in through the front door of the Estate, and slipping unobserved into my room, I locked my bedroom door closed. I dropped to the floor, in front of my personal altar, sobbing with grief. I prayed to Guru Ram Das, I prayed to that sense of God, the all-powerful presence that I felt through my meditation and prayers. I pleaded to be relieved of the pain, the sadness, the burden, the loneliness. I begged to be guided to do the right thing, to be granted the strength to carry on with my duties. Emotionally exhausted, I fell into an early sleep.

A Game of Chess

THE NEXT MORNING, at about 5am my phone rang. I uttered the words 'Sat Nam' and Siri Brahma's response was a mirror of my own, our voices equally heavy with sadness, with resignation. We shared silence for a few moments. Then I began to basically repeat what he'd already read in the note I left for him: "It's like I warned you. I was afraid this would happen. He wouldn't budge, and now we won't be allowed to see each other at all. He wasn't even going to let me tell you this myself. But I didn't agree to that."

He gently, pleadingly, interrupted me, "Please, you need to come and talk to me in person. Please don't just tell me this over the phone. I'm in Malibu right now. I couldn't go to sadhana this morning, I was too upset. Could you please just drive out here and talk to me?" He was calling me from a payphone in the parking lot at his favorite surfing spot.

I was hesitant, but I did agree with him that we needed to have face-to-face closure. Heavy-hearted, I left the Estate, headed down Robertson Boulevard, taking the familiar on-ramp to the Santa Monica Freeway. From there it was a short drive to the Pacific Coast Highway. I lowered my window, allowing the fresh ocean air to help clear my head as I drove along in the early morning quiet.

Pulling off the highway and into the parking area, I spotted Siri Brahma, his chin resting on his hands, lying on the sand and facing towards me, towards the parking lot. His surfboard lay on the ground next to him. Instead of standing up to greet me, he barely lifted his head, just watching me as I walked toward him, trudging heavily through the sand.

I was wearing my running shoes. I didn't plan to stay long.

I sat down on a large driftwood log, a few feet away from him, facing toward the ocean. Glancing sideways, I could see that his hair was still wet, tied up on top of his head. He was wearing his dark blue wetsuit top and surfing trunks. It was early spring in Southern California, and the ocean currents were still cold this time of year.

We each remained silent for a while, letting ourselves settle into a new, painful reality. I was the first one to speak, slowly and deliberately, "As I started to explain on the phone, he wouldn't even consider our request to arrange things. He says no one would be able to accept it, and my reputation would be ruined. He didn't agree that he could get Sat Kaur to accept it. I did get him to promise that he'll leave you alone, that he won't push you out of the community. Anyway, I'm just here to let you know that I did agree to stay on as Secretary General, so I won't be going away, for now."

Siri Brahma remained lying on the sand, his chin resting on his hands. He hadn't moved since I arrived. He was still facing away from the ocean, eyes still directed toward the parking lot. He hadn't said anything in response to my report, barely even looking at me, mostly just staring straight ahead. As I finished my last sentence, I looked over and saw his expression change. I saw fear and disbelief wash over him. As I turned to follow his gaze, I saw her: Siri Brahma's wife, Sat Kaur, was walking toward us. *Oh my God*, I felt my stomach drop all the way to my feet. *What was she doing here?*

Even from a distance, I could see that Sat Kaur's face was flushed bright red with anger. Her determined body-language matched her expression. She kept striding toward us as I stood up to meet her.

But there was no meeting, rather she was spewing rage and anger at me. Finger-pointing and arm waving, she began a tirade of name-calling and accusations, 'You bitch, you whore, who do you think you are? You think you are so high and mighty, the big deal Secretary General, so you can try to steal anybody's husband?'

My years of life on a pedestal had not prepared me for such verbal abuse. I could never have imagined anyone speaking to me this way. I tried to quiet her down, "Please, Sat Kaur, calm down. There's nothing to be so upset about. I was just telling Siri Brahma good-bye. We won't be seeing each other again. If you could just calm down and talk with me, there's no need for yelling and name-calling."

Barely acknowledging my plea, she continued, "I don't need to talk with you. You think you are so superior, so special that you can make your own rules? You think you can just go after any man you want? You are just a bitch, who calls herself the Secretary General. You are a disgrace."

Throughout this exchange, while her swearing and accusations continued, I had begun to trudge back toward my car, desperate to escape what had turned into a nightmare. As I moved through the deep sand, Sat Kaur and Siri Brahma were both following along close behind me. Although she was a practicing psychotherapist, my pleas for reason and calm were falling on deaf ears. Escaping from her seemed to be my only option.

Emotionally, I was feeling as though the earth beneath my feet had opened up and I was falling into a bottomless abyss. I felt groundless, with nowhere to stand, psychically, emotionally, within my own skin—no solid footing whatsoever.

I knew that Sat Kaur finding us here had changed everything. The power had just been shifted. I instinctively understood that Yogi Bhajan would consider yesterday's agreements with me null and void. And if this was what she would say to my face, imagine what she would say to everyone else in the community?

I finally inched my way past the ranting, jealous wife and into my car. At first, I rolled the window down, still trying to calm her, reason with her and coax her out of my way. Then I closed it again, to give myself some space from her continuing verbal assault. *Why would she be so angry, so abusive to me? Why would she call me such horrible names, and come to such conclusions, just seeing us sitting on the beach? We weren't even sitting next to each other. And, how did she know we were here in the first place?*

Of course! Siri Brahma must have told her where he was going when he left home this morning. That was pretty dumb! But why did she suspect anything between us? Because the Yogi must have told her—in spite of his promise to me.

As obvious as that fact should have been, it didn't register at the time, because I was in shock, consumed by feelings of shame, deep shame, of being humiliated, of being found 'wrong'.

'Wrong' was a sensation that felt life-threatening to me. Up to this point in my life, a span of 40 years, my existence was oriented toward trying very hard to be right. After all, even my very birth had been ill-timed. For my 17-year old mother, and my 20-year old father, who had eloped in the face of an impending world war, my arrival nine months after their wedding night was not really expected nor welcome.

In response to that imprint, that sense of not being wanted or welcome, I had lived my life attempting to become right. Always a good girl, a pleaser, always the teacher's pet. When none of my worldly strategies brought me the life I was trying to create, I had sought out a spiritual teacher, to keep me safe from errors in life, to show me the right path, to somehow make me right. In service to the teacher that I found, I had been self-sacrificing while dying inside: isolated, fighting to overcome my own needs, wants and desires, while hiding behind a mythic image that served as a shield against facing and knowing my own self.

Now I was gripped by the fear of losing everything that mattered to me, on the surface, along with the disintegration of the invisible shields that had protected me from my pain. Struggling to remain calm, I maneuvered my car out of the parking space, carefully working my way past Sat Kaur, as she finally moved enough to avoid being run over. Siri Brahma was a few steps behind her. He had been silent the entire time. He had done nothing to quiet her, nothing to defend me, or us. He just stood there watching it all. He even had the audacity to sheepishly smile at me as I pulled away.

I didn't have time or presence of mind to worry about that. I was near panic, trembling as I made my way back onto the Pacific Coast Hwy. I couldn't imagine what was going to happen to me now. I only knew that this episode had changed everything. It was a 20-minute drive back to Preuss Road, back to my own room at Guru Ram Das Estate. As soon as I could get to my phone, I called the Yogi. He was teaching Tantric Yoga on the East Coast that weekend. I called the ashram where he was staying. As though he was expecting my call, he personally answered the phone, with a confident and slightly lilting tone, "Sat Nam, Premka. I understand you have been enjoying a morning at the beach?"

Yogi Bhajan had once said to me, "Premka, you must learn to play chess, so you can understand how to plan ahead, so you can know in advance what will be your opponent's next move. You need to learn to think at least five moves ahead of your adversary. This is the training needed to carry on the duties of the Secretary General."

I was in checkmate. *Was I still the Secretary General? Would I now be trashed and abandoned? Where could I go, what could I do?* I was stranded, without a safety net. I had viewed Siri Brahma as my protector, but he must have been foolish enough to tell Sat Kaur where he was going that morning. He led her right to us. Now the consequences to me could be irreparable.

The Yogi's next words pulled me back, "Premka, I told you that you must not see this man again."

"Yes, you did. And I told you that I was going to see him one more time, just to explain things to him in person, face-to-face. That's all I was doing. We were just saying good-bye. We never even came near each other."

He was quick to reply, "I understand that. Now you just keep calm, Premka. I have told Sat Kaur that I'm taking care of it, and she's not to speak with anyone about this. She will do what I tell her, so not to worry."

I wanted only to run far, far away. But there was nowhere for me to go. I had no resources. I hadn't owned my own car in 15 years. If I tried to drive off in 'my' Mercedes, I could be charged with theft since it was registered to Sikh Dharma. I had no money. In fact, like all of the staff members, I was extended out on credit cards. I was in debt, another kind of imprisonment.

The Yogi began to reassure me, "Calm down, Premka, and just listen to me. Here is what you must do. I want you to get yourself packed up and just get going to New Mexico. It's almost time for the Summer Solstice preparations anyway. You must have no contact with this Siri Brahma. Guru Ram Das is with us, not to worry. It will all be fine. I'll handle Sat Kaur, and this Siri Brahma. They'll do what I say."

For me, one of the most appealing qualities of the Yogi, was his power, his always masterful handling of situations and circumstances. When he stepped in, there was no doubt that he was in charge. I felt somewhat reassured, to hear him say that he would handle this. Apparently, I wasn't being thrown out on the street.

But I also knew that I no longer had an ounce of personal power or any standing, except for what he chose to give me. Two days earlier, I had been anticipating the taste of freedom, believing I had a partner and a plan to get there. Today I found myself trapped and headed for prison. Solitary confinement, no less.

I should have learned to play chess.

A Hollow Ghost

WHAT I MOST LOVED ABOUT TRAVELING, was the feeling of letting go, of clearing my desk, of shifting my focus, adjusting patterns and places, schedules and routines. Packing up just the essentials of my life and leaving more behind than I was taking with me, brought a welcome freedom from routine, a hint of change, the lightening up of pressures and responsibilities.

Under normal circumstances my yearly spring trip to New Mexico lifted my spirits. The high desert was elevating, as I would feel myself opening to the big, wide vistas, the brilliant blue skies that would routinely cloud over and break into awe-inspiring lightning and thunderstorms.

But this trip in the spring of 1984 was not like that. I was struggling to maintain some calm, going through the motions of packing, making reservations and boarding the aircraft, with the Yogi coaching me each step of the way. Inside, I felt my entire world coming apart.

Emotionally, long before being discovered on the beach by Sat Kaur, what I wanted to do was to break free of the Yogi. But I was also absolutely certain that I didn't want to lose my connection to the Dharma or the community. This was my family. This was the family that I had found to replace my own birth family. I lived my life for the world-changing vision we all shared, and that relationship was what defined my sense of myself. My identity was totally interwoven with the evolution of the Western Sikhs.

When Sat Kaur appeared on the beach just two days earlier,

when she shrieked at me with her red face and her arms waving, calling me obscene names, a huge crack was opened up—a crack in the glass bubble that I had accepted as my reality. It was a crack that exposed a vulnerability, the potential for my carefully crafted image, the fragile illusory shield that had served to shelter me, to shatter into a million pieces. That experience on the beach brought up guilt and shame. Ancient stuff, from other lifetimes perhaps. I felt naked, exposed and painfully vulnerable. The abyss was yawning beneath me. That sense of groundlessness would not go away.

Playing that scene over and over in my head, grappling for a solution, for resolution, I picked up my luggage from the baggage claim carousel and walked out the gate of the Albuquerque airport. I immediately spotted Sat Narayan's dark blue turban, as he leaned casually against the Yogi's cream-colored 1966 Mercedes 600, parked at curbside. Tall and good-looking, Sat Narayan was the Yogi's full-time mechanic, in charge of a veritable fleet of aging but near-classic cars.

Smiling cheerfully, innocent of my dilemma, Sat Narayan repeated the usual 'Sat Nam', as he held the passenger door open. Feeling little besides the weight of my situation, I slipped into the comfort of the oversized passenger seat, covered by the genuine sheepskin that had become standard requirement for all of the Yogi's fleet of cars. He often explained to his faithful followers, "This static electricity which happens when you step on these nylon carpets or slide across these upholstered seats, it interferes with the magnetic field. I'm too much sensitive, you know. That is the curse of being the Mahan Tantric. This sheepskin creates a natural protection against those shocks, plus it insulates from the magnetic pull of the earth."

The warmth, the sensation of being held in the soft cushioning of sheep's wool, was familiar and comforting. I pulled my seatbelt across, clicking it into place, and quickly pushed a Gurbani Kirtan music cassette into the console, hoping for some relief from the relentless activity of my mind. We mostly drove without conversation, and occasionally I rolled down the window to deeply inhale the special fragrance the intermittent rain releases when it hits the scorched desert floor. I loved that smell—a scent of release and renewal.

The drive from Albuquerque was 1½ hours long and took us across the beautiful town of Santa Fe, then further north to Espanola. We were headed to The Ranch, the 11-acre property owned by the Yogi. It was nestled in the floor of the Espanola valley, and over the years had grown into a complex of residential structures and a few mobile homes. Small dwellings were ever-proliferating on The Ranch, in order to house his immediate family as well as the increasing number of staff members needed to help manage the major events held throughout the summer.

Many of these small residential facilities had been built on top of the crumbling foundations of old out-buildings, and storage sheds from the previous owners. My personal residence was one of those structures. It had once been a slaughterhouse, for sheep. (The irony of this did not escape me.) It was an oddly proportioned little structure, shaped like a miniature house with a peaked roof, but with extra high exterior walls (to accommodate the ramp once provided for those ill-fated sheep.) These 15-foot walls now accommodated a low-clearance sleeping loft set above clothes closets.

My tiny cottage had been remodeled and furnished by the head of the Espanola ashram (Wha Guru Singh) and the talented and devoted artisans of this community. It was fully carpeted in a sunny shade of yellow, with hand-painted dark blue and white Mexican tiles inlaid around all the windows and doors. There was a sitting area at the entry that measured barely eight feet square. A large, Mexican-tiled bathroom with a custom-built sunken tub had been added to the original structure. There was no kitchen.

I had previously loved this little private cottage of mine, but this year it was my cave, where I cried most of the days and nights throughout that long summer. I was consumed by fear, shame and guilt all dovetailing into a familiar feeling of hopeless despair. Sometimes I managed to sit and pray or meditate in front of the altar in my loft. Now and then some staff member would be sent to check on me, maybe offer me a foot massage, or the Yogi might summon me to a meal at the main ranch-house. When he called for me, reluctantly I would pull myself together, get properly dressed and walk up to the main house.

I wanted to see no one, rather I wanted no one to see me. Whenever I was pressured into attending some event, or the Sunday morning Gurdwara, I felt as though my forehead was imprinted with a scarlet letter, as though the only thing anyone could see was my wrong-ness. In reality, not many people really knew what was going on, and they outwardly behaved normally toward me. However, I was suffering from massive internal judgments, voices coming at me from every side, repeating a familiar theme: *Wrong— not right!* The imprints from my own conception and birth were possessing me, a birth that was not intended. My early indoctrination into Christian beliefs about original sin had provided an additional layer to my youthful sense of wrongness. Now all of that early imprint was activated, and all of the unconscious beliefs and assumptions were bombarding my psyche. Nonetheless, I was also conditioned to keep up appearances, to carry on with my duties.

Thankfully, I had an experienced and effective team in place for handling the many logistical aspects of the summer's large events. The Summer Solstice celebration at the nearby Guru Ram Das Puri, had an attendance that year of nearly 1200 students from around the world. As necessary, I met with my team leaders overseeing everything from sanitation and fresh food deliveries, to the care of young children and medical emergencies. In order to avoid appearing in public any more than necessary, I arranged to have the registration income delivered to me in my cottage, on a daily basis. I found some relief via the practical task of counting money and adding up receipts. The simple, straightforward logic of addition and subtraction was comforting. The constancy of numbers was a relief from the tumultuous activity of my mind and emotions.

I had no further contact with Siri Brahma over that summer of 1984. I mailed back the key to our post office box. No message. Just the key. That was my message.

Whenever the Yogi would speak privately with me, he would offer unsolicited reports, "I have asked Sat Kaur to report to me on a daily basis about all of this Siri Brahma's activities. I have told her to give me a psychological profile of this guy, which you will be interested to hear. By the way, you might also like to know that Siri Brahma is sleeping on the living room floor these days."

I learned that he was now forbidden to enter Guru Ram Das ashram. He had been informed that he was not allowed to attend morning sadhana or Sunday services. As I had anticipated, the Yogi no longer felt any obligation to honor that earlier agreement we had made. I listened, asking no questions, making no comments. I was resigned to whatever he was doing, to whatever was going to happen. I no longer felt that I had control over any of it. My opinions or suggestions were neither invited nor welcome.

I felt like a hollow ghost, sitting through dinners or evening gatherings around Yogi Bhajan. Thankfully, my pain seemed to be invisible to everyone around me. We were all well trained to ignore each other's meltdowns, effectively imprinting the habit of denial on our psyches. Besides, no one ever really talked to each other around the Yogi. He always held center stage, as his staff members and volunteers rotated in and out of the room with his food, his special drinks, his vitamins, his remedies that had been recommended by any number of healing practitioners.

By now he was technically obese and dealing with issues like high blood pressure and diabetes. Someone was usually sitting at the foot of his recliner chair, massaging his feet. Everyone would listen to his commentaries on the political issues of the day, or he might share oft-repeated stories of his athletic prowess as a college rugby player or re-tell the story of leading his village out of Pakistan to India during the Partition. Or he might just fall asleep. In that event, a designated attendant would appear and encourage everyone to quietly depart.

I was more of an observer than ever. Isolated within my own fearful world, I worried about Siri Brahma and how he would react to the pressure. I wondered how it was that Sat Kaur didn't realize that spying on her husband and reporting on him to his teacher was sure to push him away? I wondered if Yogi Bhajan thought that this was really a way to teach him a lesson? It made no sense to me. Normally great efforts were made to keep people in the Dharma. Now I prayed that Siri Brahma wouldn't let Yogi Bhajan's tactics push him all the way out, that he wouldn't take off his turban and leave in the dead of night. I couldn't bear to think that our relationship would be the cause of his departure from the Dharma, from the Guru.

I didn't know what people might be thinking, what the other staff members knew, what the rumors might be. Throughout my life I had been a pleaser, a good girl, striving for some imagined perfection, seeking love and acceptance. Now the image I had effectively hidden behind was being shattered. Instead, I was facing my own truths, apart from anybody else's expectations. I was reviewing my willingness to step up to the role my teacher had defined for me: "Premka, you must just be me. You must not be this little you. You must not be emotional; you cannot be a woman at all. You are to become me. Then you can just carry on when I'm gone. That's what is needed."

From the earliest years of serving Yogi Bhajan, I had found it easy to channel him, to write letters on his behalf. In fact, I had gained an amazing level of notoriety among Indian Sikhs for a lengthy letter that I once wrote at his instigation. That letter was subsequently made into a small pamphlet, entitled 'The Rejoinder' and re-printed in the tens of thousands (by the SGPC, the administrative body for the Sikhs of India) for distribution throughout Sikh congregations in India and even beyond, to Singapore, Malaysia, England and Canada.

I was now acknowledging to myself that I could never be him. More than that, I was facing the fact that, even if it were possible, I didn't **want** to be him. I had reached my personal limits. I wanted to be me. Throughout my entire life, right up to this moment, I had felt a gap, a painful sense of separation between my inner sense of myself and the rest of the world. I virtually always felt like an outsider, like an observer or even an imposter.

Now, in the face of all the judgmental voices bombarding me, I was concluding that the role Yogi Bhajan had been defining for me, the one where I was supposed to be him, was not in alignment with my own inner truth, with my own inner knowing. Having no one and nothing else to turn to, I was discovering my own guidance. At that time, I had no tools, training or support for such self-awareness. I might not have been able to identify or articulate the discernment that was being made. It guided me nonetheless.

I didn't have the answers about what I could do next, for how to move on. There were many practical questions left to be resolved. The good news was, in the midst of all the torturous soul-searching, I was beginning to stand on firmer ground, within my own being.

In exile, we must do as the goddess Innana did, surrendering layer after layer of armor and adornment, until we are bare. We must then undergo a symbolic death of the old life in order to be reborn with greater resilience and a holy assignment to carry forward. The initiated adult has learned to withstand uncertainty, has paid a debt to the gods through his loss and his grief, and has decided to make beauty with his life as the future ancestor that he is.

~ Excerpt from *Belonging: Remembering Ourselves Home* by TOKO-PA TURNER (belongingbook.com)

Synchronicity

IT WAS NEARLY FOUR MONTHS since my rushed departure to New Mexico, when along with other staff members, I finally returned to Los Angeles. I was physically back, but I was not at all sure I could continue on with the status quo. I made my daily appearance at my office in the Secretariat, dealing with whatever tasks were in front of me. I lived with a heavy, nauseating sensation in my gut, accompanied by the terrifying awareness that nothing would ever be normal again. I could not go back in time, I could not reclaim my prior innocence. I could not pretend that none of the events of last spring had ever happened.

I also felt a tangible sense of betrayal by Yogi Bhajan. I barely recognized it at the time, because I was overwhelmed by self-condemnation. But he was surely responsible for Sat Kaur's appearance on the beach in Malibu. There was no other reason for her anger and accusations.

Now he had taken complete control of the unfolding of events around that story: He censored and effectively excommunicated Siri Brahma; he kept Sat Kaur reporting to him on a regular basis, keeping her occupied and feeling important. He regularly reported to me, observing my aura, my reactions, while making me feel somewhat safe and secure, as though nothing had really changed.

I was still there, still the Secretary General, still apparently his confidante. But I could never be convinced of that. Deep down, I knew that nothing would ever be the same.

One afternoon, shortly after my return to Los Angeles, I was driving up Preuss Road when I spotted Siri Brahma pulling up to the front of Guru Ram Das ashram on his motorcycle. Although he saw me as I passed in front of him, he looked away without a word or a sign. His expression appeared heavy, resigned and angry. I recognized that he was feeling his own sense of betrayal. I wished I could reach out to him and try to offer more explanation. I desperately wanted to fix everything, take away his pain, heal all the wounds that had been inflicted. But I was in no position to offer him anything.

It was just a few days later when I was scheduled to drive Yogi Bhajan to one of his many doctor appointments. As we pulled away from the curb and out onto a moderately busy Robertson Boulevard, we both spotted Siri Brahma. He was pulling a basket of clothes from the bed of his truck, carrying it into the neighborhood laundromat. The Yogi took the opportunity to prod me, "Ah, Premka, there is the great love of your life, doing his laundry. Maybe we should stop and you can just tell him how much you are in love with him now."

Shock and rage swept through me. Keeping my left hand firmly on the steering wheel, with my right hand I took hold of my neatly folded pashmina shawl ,the one trimmed with a row of colorfully embroidered hookah-smoking Mughals, and I lashed out at him with that soft shawl striking him across the side of his face as I raged, "Unbelievable! You're disgusting and cruel. You mock love, and you play games with peoples' lives. And you think that's okay? Well, I don't think so." Briefly, I saw a look of shock cross his face, but he instantly covered it with a false and mocking grin.

That outburst of rage even surprised me. For the entire summer, I had been holding back a flood of resentment and anger, accepting my shame and my punishment. I had remained silent and passive, feeling literally bound and gagged as I witnessed the Yogi moving the lives of the people around him, like pawns on a chessboard. I had been a silent, non-protesting witness as he played his all-powerful role as the spiritual teacher in the lives of his followers.

His inner circle witnessed along with me, and I saw how they applauded and found God's Will as well as humor in the Yogi's decisions to upend lives, to marry people to strangers, to send young children away from their parents to schools in India. With every individual appointment, and every life turned upside down, the faithful ones in that inner circle would knowingly nod and smile, then repeat the mantra that 'It's all God's Will'. To my pained and more cynical eyes, this 'God's Will' was now looking tainted, and highly suspect.

I drove Yogi Bhajan to his doctor's appointment that morning. His high blood pressure was once again confirmed, and instructions regarding diet and medications were passed along to me as his attendant of the moment. In the car, we filled the heavy silence between us with cassette tapes of Gurbani Kirtan. The Yogi was aggressively fingering the beads of his pearl mala, while his rapid eye movements betrayed his busily computing mind.

Once I had safely delivered him back to Guru Ram Das ashram, I drove the two long blocks up the street lined with Jacaranda trees, heading for my room at the Estate. There I contemplated what I had done, my shocking and almost violent outburst. I realized that I didn't care anymore. I didn't care about holding up my image. I didn't care to pretend (at least to myself) that I trusted or believed in the Yogi's pure motivations.

But there was still a huge hook—the entire community. To walk away from Yogi Bhajan would potentially mean losing everything I loved, everything that mattered to me: the community, the lifestyle, the Guru, the Dharma, position, title, financial security, everything!

Yogi Bhajan was typically quick to present a new and dark public portrait of anyone who chose to carve out their own path. I had been there for the loss of some of my most cherished members of the Khalsa Council, like Wha Guru Singh and Guru Shabd Singh, heads of large communities in Espanola and the Boston area. I also saw how the community so easily embraced their teacher's revised versions of people and events.

I could only hope and pray that he would want to uphold my image, that I was as important to the future of the community as he always claimed.

The next day, after a long and restless night, I called him on his private line. "I'm calling to tell you, for the final time, that I'm leaving the staff. I'm resigning as Secretary General and will no longer live in your household. I want to have a normal life, living in an ashram community just like any other Sikh. I'd like to move to either San Diego or Eugene and would like to work on other writing projects there. It can be a smooth transition, if you want to help orchestrate it. No matter what, I'm leaving your household."

There was dead silence for a second or two, before he responded, "I see, Premka. By the way, did you know that Siri Brahma came to see me today? He has informed me that he is getting a divorce from Sat Kaur."

It had been four months since I had exchanged a single word with Siri Brahma. What synchronicity! We had both arrived at our independent decisions, on the exact same day. My mind rapidly consumed with hopeful possibilities, I thoughtfully replied, "No, I didn't know that."

The synchronicity of our separate decisions felt to me like a sign from the universe, encouragement to honor the urgings of my heart.

Within minutes of hanging up from that phone call with Yogi Bhajan, I sent a message to Siri Brahma. A few hours later, we were reunited and confirmed our continuing desire to build a life together.

Over the next few weeks, we had various meetings with the Yogi, because Siri Brahma and I were both committed to maintaining our Sikh identities and our connection to the greater community of Sikhs. That seemed to me to be a logical and desirable outcome for all concerned. It still made sense to me that the Yogi would want that.

He did work with us on a game plan, but it included his insistence that we must move off the North American continent, "You must establish yourself far away from everyone, to give time for the community to accept that Premka, the Secretary General, is getting married with an ordinary man."

I disagreed with his premise, "Sir, I think people in this community would be happy to see me have an ordinary householder's life. I think they would love to see me married. I understand it could look scandalous, but the truth is that you created the circumstance by marrying Siri Brahma to Sat Kaur. And you could easily cover for us."

Instead, his idea was that Siri Brahma could go to Guam and establish a school for the children of our community. Up to now, such a school had been situated in India, but the Yogi claimed to be looking for another alternative. Meanwhile, we agreed that a Proclamation would be issued regarding my resignation as Secretary General and my move to the Eugene ashram to carry on with translation work on Yogi Bhajan's poetry.

Soon I flew to Eugene, Oregon to begin my transition out of Los Angeles, while Siri Brahma went to check out Guam. In our first conversation from Guam, Siri Brahma was clear in his observations, "No, we do not want to move to Guam. It's a very small island and flat and it is primarily a military base. Plus, they have a big problem here—brown snakes! When you open the kitchen cupboards, they are crawling with brown snakes! It's not a place we would ever want to live."

He had other thoughts to share: "I'm thinking about Hawaii. I lived and worked there before, so I'm going to make a stop on the way back to Los Angeles, so I can check out whether it would be feasible to move there. I have old friends and work connections on Oahu."

The Yogi was insisting that I remain in Eugene for at least six months while the divorce was finalized 'in order to avoid scandal'. But I had observed Yogi Bhajan for 16 years and I knew how his mind worked. I understood that the Guam trip had simply been a diversionary tactic. I knew that if he could keep him busy at a distance, he would be relentless in trying to drive a wedge between me and Siri Brahma. He was hoping to have six months to wear me down. And, quite honestly, I was concerned for Siri Brahma's physical safety. The Yogi had a long reach!

Meanwhile, just stepping away from Los Angeles and the Secretariat and the circle surrounding the Yogi, I was growing increasingly energized at the prospect of the freedom I was anticipating—freedom to be an ordinary person, to achieve a kind of anonymity.

In late November of 1984, balmy and flower-scented breezes greeted me as I disembarked from my Hawaiian Air Lines flight at Honolulu airport. Siri Brahma was there to receive me with a radiant smile that mirrored my own, as he placed a fragrant lei over my turbaned head and hugged me openly, in front of the whole wide world.

Healing Time
(Epilogue)

H AWAII IS A PLACE OF HEALING for many who seek out the gentle comforts of her tropical climate, warm oceans and the replenishing breezes that keep her vitalized. I have been one of these. Siri Brahma and I did get married in a Sikh ceremony six months after leaving the North American continent, in May of 1985. Our son, Casey Dyson, was born on November 20th of 1986.

With my arrival in Hawaii, the biggest awakenings of my own spiritual journey were just beginning. I had stepped off my pedestal and into life as an ordinary person, on an island where almost nobody knew me. Although I continued to wear my turban for a time, I also began to wear more ordinary clothes as encouraged by the weather and the lifestyle of Hawaii; which naturally included bathing suits with a wrapped sarong for a skirt. It was delicious to just be myself, still devoted to the Sikh faith, with a husband who shared the same devotion and commitment.

Then within weeks, and over the ensuing months, via the infamous 3HO wireless, I began to hear new stories, new descriptions of Premka. These were the latest stories the Yogi was telling, a new version of me: fallen woman/harlot and traitor. I heard that he lamented to his followers that I had 'fallen to my second chakra'. He was subtly and systematically deconstructing my image, the myth of Premka, in order to explain my departure from his staff and to ultimately discredit me in the eyes of his followers. Damage control was under way.

It would be difficult to explain the depth of my pain. This

abandonment was as devastating to me as if I had passed through a war and lost everything and everyone. Most painful of all, it was being orchestrated by the one I had entrusted with my spiritual destiny.

The Yogi had been so many things to me, for 16 years of my adult life: guru, spiritual teacher, provider, lover, father, and essentially God. The community that grew up around us had replaced my own family of origin. Now virtually all of them seemed to be abandoning me and accepting a new version of me. As a result, I experienced the loss of my teacher, the loss of my community, loss of my family, loss of my identity, loss of my religious path and loss of financial security. After devoting the prime years of my adult life to the building of the organization and the community, I was cut off and left with nothing.

Being the recipient of a new identity, this new dark projection, helped to clarify the previous exalted image as well. I came to realize a much deeper truth, that neither of these outer identities was what was ultimately true, or real. With this insight, greater space was realized, within myself. I was not this, nor that. Indeed, I learned to sense a deeper and more spacious connection to my own True Nature. I learned to meditate in silence, in stillness, and to be guided by the inner compass that had always been there, quietly leading me through my entire life journey.

Throughout the next years of my transition, everything the Yogi had ever taught me, my entire spiritual path, began to be deeply questioned. My life was my spiritual path, and my life was teaching me.

In the face of so much disillusionment and the accompanying sense of betrayal, I was also grappling with my concept of God, and my attachment to the Sikh faith. Through years of therapy, meditation and internal examination, I began to discriminate out the subtle fact that I had made the unconscious error of perceiving

God as something outside of myself. The Sikh scriptures say repeatedly, that 'God is within. Guru is within'. I loved that teaching, and in theory, I believed it was the truth. Yet the very practice of bowing before the scripture or adhering to the guidance of a teacher instead of being encouraged to look within, and even the use of the word God, all subtly reinforced an outer orientation, an illusion of separateness.

I also came to see the ways this implied separation was reinforced by the lifestyle and practices within the community. For one thing, we had a dress code which served to create a highly visible separation from the rest of society, along with beliefs about the superiority of that lifestyle and dress code. We were taught to physically bow before God and Guru on a daily basis—a God and Guru that are thus demonstrably externalized. We were taught to practice an ideal of surrendering to the guidance of the Yogi, the spiritual teacher, rather than being encouraged to seek out our own intuition or inner voice. There was also a not-so-subtle class-consciousness that was built into the structure of the community, with layers of titles and inner circles, access to the teacher, etc.

Separation is an illusion, perhaps the ultimate illusion. I began to recognize the reinforcement of this illusion as the quintessential misconception. It was also the source of the pain that drove me to go within. I ultimately developed my capacity to sense the pain, the hurt and abandonment and to stay with that pain long enough to let it speak to me. The Diamond Approach[23] teachings and techniques taught me to sense its location within my body; within my heart, my throat, my chest, wherever it was experienced.

---

23 Diamond Approach www.diamondapproach.org

I learned to stay with it and to look at it with gentle curiosity, allowing it to inform me. I discovered that this process transformed the identification with the pain, releasing its grip, so I could see behind its illusory nature. In its place, I discovered spaciousness, emptiness, the All That Is.

I am grateful for my unique journey with all of its amazing twists and turns. I often remind myself that if I had not had these lessons to learn, they would not have come to me.

Acknowledgments

MY WRITING CIRCLE ON MAUI, facilitated by Jasmyne Boswell, was the entry point into the deep introspection that brought this book forth. I am grateful for the thoughtful and consistent feedback she provided, helping me learn creative ways to express my stories.

The friendships that grew from that Writing Circle and their ongoing enthusiasm and encouragement over the years was invaluable, including Maribeth Thiesen, Peter Mellen, Martie Geltz, Helen Kritzler (Haiku Helen).

Then there are my dear ones who were there with me, back when the events of this story were taking place, and who have continued to be friends and supporters. These include Tej Steiner who has been my friend and brother over so many years, Antion Vikram Singh and Elandra who have been major cheer leaders, Kamalla who threatened to write my story if I didn't, Soorya Kaur, John Lamenzo, Jack Dyson (aka Siri Brahma) and our son, Casey Dyson.

My great appreciation for Rebecca Walker, published author and writing coach. She gave me highly insightful input about my key challenge: to keep this story as my own.

Katharine Hartwig Dahl, a dear sister and magical being who recently served to ignite my creativity once again, to finally complete this work.

Last but certainly not least, there is my life partner, Russell Welch. Over more than 10 years of my processing and writing, he has been my hero. A loving partner, he always afforded me the time and space to bring the story forth, while consistently believing in me, and in the power of my story.

About the Author

WITHIN MONTHS OF HIS ARRIVAL in the United States, Pamela attended her first semi-private yoga class with Yogi Bhajan. He quickly swept her into service as his driver, photographer, personal attendant and secretary. He was one of the many Eastern-born teachers who appeared in the U.S. in the midst of the transformational '60s.

Over the course of the next 16 years, re-naming her Premka, Yogi Bhajan called upon her innate abilities, encouraging her to document the growth of their proliferating lifestyle community and the evolution of individuals from New Agers to yogis and finally to Sikhs. She became the Administrative Director for the International Headquarters of 3HO Foundation and Sikh Dharma International and the first Secretary General for the international ministerial council of the Sikhs (Khalsa Council).

Premka rendered some of the major prayers of the Sikhs into American English, in a book entitled *Peace Lagoon*[24], first published in 1971. She also served as Editor of the community's 32-page quarterly magazine, entitled *Beads of Truth*. In 1979, she

[24] *Peace Lagoon*, Sardarni Premka Kaur Khalsa, 1971

helped to conceptualize, compile and edit a full color volume of more than 400 pages, presenting a history of Yogi Bhajan's achievements in the U.S. The volume was a gift in honor of his 50th birthday and was entitled *The Man Called the Siri Singh Sahib*[25].

In 1984, she moved to Hawaii, married Siri Brahma (Jack Dyson) and within two years, their son Casey Dyson, was born. Over the course of the ten years of their marriage, they designed and built a total of five houses and flipped a few fixer-uppers as well.

Like many women, her time out of the workplace impacted her career skills: she had missed the transition to computers and the internet. When it was time to step back into full time employment, she chose to move in a totally different direction, going back to school to become licensed as a massage therapist, while writing her stories and providing editing and proofreading services.

Pamela currently lives in upcountry Maui. She and her partner of the past 15 years raise chickens and honeybees plus freshwater fish and vegetables in an aquaponics greenhouse. Utilizing catchment water and solar electricity, they strive to live in greater harmony with the beautiful nature that surrounds them.

[25] *The Man Called the Siri Singh Sahib*, Sardarni Premka Kaur Khalsa and Sat Kirpal Kaur Khalsa, 1979

CPSIA information can be obtained
at www.ICGtesting.com
Printed in the USA
BVHW032052310320
576533BV00001B/152